Managing Student Affairs Effectively

M. Lee Upcraft, Margaret J. Barr, *Editors*

NEW DIRECTIONS FOR STUDENT SERVICES

MARGARET J. BARR, *Editor-in-Chief*
Texas Christian University

M. LEE UPCRAFT, *Associate Editor*
Pennsylvania State University

Number 41, Spring 1988

Paperback sourcebooks in
The Jossey-Bass Higher Education Series

Jossey-Bass Inc., Publishers
San Francisco • London

M. Lee Upcraft, Margaret J. Barr (eds.).
Managing Student Affairs Effectively.
New Directions for Student Services, no. 41.
San Francisco: Jossey-Bass, 1988.

New Directions for Student Services
Margaret J. Barr, *Editor-in-Chief;* M. Lee Upcraft, *Associate Editor*

New Directions for Student Services is published quarterly
by Jossey-Bass Inc., Publishers (publication number USPS
449-070). Second-class postage paid at San Francisco, California, and at
additional mailing offices. POSTMASTER: Send address changes
to Jossey-Bass Inc., Publishers, 350 Sansome Street, San Francisco,
California 94104.

Editorial correspondence should be sent to the Editor-in-Chief,
Margaret J. Barr, Sadler Hall, Texas Christian University,
Fort Worth, Texas 76129.

Library of Congress Catalog Card Number LC 85-644751

International Standard Serial Number ISSN 0164-7970

International Standard Book Number ISBN 1-55542-926-2

Cover art by WILLI BAUM

Manufactured in the United States of America

Ordering Information

The paperback sourcebooks listed below are published quarterly and can be ordered either by subscription or single copy.

Subscriptions cost $48.00 per year for institutions, agencies, and libraries. Individuals can subscribe at the special rate of $36.00 per year *if payment is by personal check.* (Note that the full rate of $48.00 applies if payment is by institutional check, even if the subscription is designated for an individual.) Standing orders are accepted.

Single copies are available at $11.95 when payment accompanies order. (California, New Jersey, New York, and Washington, D.C., residents please include appropriate sales tax.) For billed orders, cost per copy is $11.95 plus postage and handling.

Substantial discounts are offered to organizations and individuals wishing to purchase bulk quantities of Jossey-Bass sourcebooks. Please inquire.

Please note that these prices are for the academic year 1987–88 and are subject to change without notice. Also, some titles may be out of print and therefore not available for sale.

To ensure correct and prompt delivery, all orders must give either the *name of an individual* or an *official purchase order number.* Please submit your order as follows:

Subscriptions: specify series and year subscription is to begin.
Single Copies: specify sourcebook code (such as, SS1) and first two words of title.

Mail orders for United States and Possessions, Latin America, Canada, Japan, Australia, and New Zealand to:
    Jossey-Bass Inc., Publishers
    350 Sansome Street
    San Francisco, California 94104

Mail orders for all other parts of the world to:
    Jossey-Bass Limited
    28 Banner Street
    London EC1Y 8QE

New Directions for Student Services Series
Margaret J. Barr, *Editor-in-Chief;* M. Lee Upcraft, *Associate Editor*

Contents

Editors' Notes

Most student affairs managers learn how to manage through experience, with successes and failures guiding their learning on a day-by-day basis. This sourcebook synthesizes what the authors have learned and found useful in more than two decades of successes and failures at all levels of student affairs management. It is intended as a nuts and bolts approach to the management of people and resources in student affairs, emphasizing practical advice for handling the daily issues and problems that student affairs managers face. Middle- and upper-level student affairs managers and those aspiring to such positions will find this volume particularly useful.

For the purposes of this sourcebook, *student affairs management* is defined as "the process of organizing available human and fiscal resources to meet institutional and program goals in an efficient, effective, ethical, and fiscally responsible manner." This sourcebook focuses on all of these elements of management from the practitioner's point of view. It is not intended to be an in-depth, theoretical treatment of student affairs management.

In Chapter One, Margaret J. Barr describes the context of higher education in the United States, provides a working definition of management, and describes the unique management problems faced by student affairs managers. She identifies methods for planning and goal setting, and offers several rules for improving managerial effectiveness.

In Chapter Two, Barr focuses on fiscal management and budgetary skills essential to effective student affairs management. She distinguishes between fiscal management in public and private institutions, and identifies several sources of funds. She discusses capital budgeting, offers strategies for funding new programs, and gives advice on building budgets within student affairs. The chapter concludes with several simple yet useful rules for getting and keeping fiscal resources.

In Chapter Three, M. Lee Upcraft offers advice on how to manage staff in a way that maintains high productivity and high morale. He identifies the problems student affairs professionals encounter as managers and offers a four-step process for managing people: (1) recruiting and selecting the right people, (2) orienting and training new employees, (3) supervising for both high productivity and high morale, and (4) evaluating performance.

In Chapter Four, Barr offers advice on how to manage key constituency groups important to the success of the student affairs manager, including students, their parents and family members, faculty, other

1

administrative staff, governing boards, and community members. Perhaps more important, she suggests how to manage the "boss," and how to become a good campus politician. She concludes by offering guidelines for managing important others.

In Chapter Five, Upcraft offers advice on the difficult task of managing in the best interests of students, the institution, and staff. He identifies the management ethics, personal values, and intuitive judgment necessary to manage "right." He concludes by suggesting ways in which controversial decisions should be managed to minimize conflict and resistance.

In Chapter Six, Barr and Upcraft summarize the management principles presented in this sourcebook and present an annotated bibliography of selected references for student affairs managers.

We recognize that offering straightforward advice about complex management problems and issues based on our own successes and failures is risky. There are bound to be professionals whose experiences have led them to different conclusions. We acknowledge that risk and hope that at a minimum, the agreements and disagreements about our points of view will generate discussion and further research into student affairs management.

M. Lee Upcraft
Margaret J. Barr
Editors

M. Lee Upcraft is assistant vice-president for counseling and health services and affiliate associate professor of education at the Pennsylvania State University. He is also associate editor of the New Directions for Student Services *sourcebooks in the Jossey-Bass higher education series. He has written and edited books and journal articles on alcohol education, orientation, the freshman year experience, and the selection and training of resident assistants.*

Margaret J. Barr is vice-chancellor for student affairs at Texas Christian University and former vice-president for student affairs at Northern Illinois University. She is a former president of the American College Personnel Association (ACPA), has been elected as a senior scholar for ACPA, and is a former recipient of the Professional Service Award of ACPA. She has also received the award for Outstanding Contribution to Literature and Research from the National Association of Student Personnel Administrators (NASPA). She is author of over twenty publications, including Developing Effective Student Services Programs *(Jossey-Bass, 1985), with L. A. Keating, and is editor-in-chief of* New Directions for Student Services.

The ability to understand and apply management principles is a central skill in student affairs administration.

Managing the Enterprise

Margaret J. Barr

In order to discuss student affairs management in a responsible way, it is necessary to understand the complex, variable, and dynamic nature of the enterprise. Consider a typical day of the chief student affairs officer on any campus. Put yourself in his or her shoes for just a few seconds and think about what happens upon walking into the office in the morning. The following expected and unexpected events may unfold.

- A regular meeting of the executive cabinet of the institution is scheduled to determine the final budget guidelines for the institution in the next fiscal year.
- An irate father calls to complain about the conflict his daughter is having with her roommate and to let you know how uncooperative the housing staff has been in dealing with the issue.
- An agency director arrives for a regular supervisory meeting and asks for help in dealing with a very difficult personnel problem.
- A student whom you met at a recent campus event calls in tears and asks to see you today.
- An insurance salesman calls to inquire about getting on the bid list for the student insurance program.
- The president's office forwards ten pieces of correspondence for you to handle.
- Another agency director arrives for a regular conference, and you find he has not completed a crucial staff assignment.

M. L. Upcraft and M. J. Barr (eds.). *Managing Student Affairs Effectively.*
New Directions for Student Services, no. 41. San Francisco: Jossey-Bass, Spring 1988.

- A student calls to ask you to judge the homecoming parade.
- A faculty member calls expressing concern about the behavior of a student in his class.
- The vice-president for development calls to ask you to make a speech for an important alumni group.
- The first draft of a report on campus security is due in the president's office today for review before being sent to members of the governing board.
- A staff member calls to tell you about a hazing incident that occurred last night.

Of course, the list of tasks to accomplish, decisions to be made, and action to be taken on any one day could even be longer and more complex than this one; on other days, the list could be shorter. But the activities, events, and crises described above will not be startling to those in charge of student affairs units. They typify the environment within which student affairs administrators must live, work, and manage the resources entrusted to their care.

Student affairs professionals typically take great pride in the services and programs they offer on their campuses, and that pride is often justified. If, however, the programs, activities, and services offered by student affairs managers are handled inefficiently and ineffectively, then their good intentions may be for naught. For example, there may be skilled counselors in the mental health unit, but if students have to wait weeks for help, the skills of those counselors do not make any difference in campus life at the institution. Student affairs staff may be warm and caring, but if students are living in less than adequate conditions, the sincerity of that care is questioned. Officers may develop and implement outstanding programs, but if the budget is always in the red, their judgment will be questioned. In short, student affairs administrators must be sound and effective managers as well as specialists in their field.

Acquiring and using management skills is often complicated by how professionals perceive themselves. Over the years, there has been a debate within the student affairs profession over whether they should be considered student development *specialists* or *administrators*. Ambler (1980) argues that such debates are unproductive and unnecessary. He states that it is necessary, although not in itself sufficient, for student affairs professionals to become sound managers. Other roles can flow from this baseline competency.

This chapter is designed to aid student affairs professionals to expand their thinking about management of the student affairs enterprise. Although the examples used in this chapter are given from the perspective of the chief student affairs officer, the advice should be useful to agency directors and others who aspire to become administrators in higher education.

The Context of American Higher Education

American higher education is characterized by diversity, unparalleled access and opportunity, and unique governance structures (Brubacher and Rudy, 1958). The diversity of the American higher education system is unique in the world. It contains public, private, two-year, four-year, multi-purpose, single-focus, large and small, urban, coed, women's, and historically black institutions, all of which contribute to the diverse fabric of American higher education. It has evolved remarkably from the original colonial colleges, which were dedicated to the education of the aristocracy and sons of ministers. American higher education developed, in part, in response to changes in the philosophy of higher education as reflected in public policy decisions and societal expectations. Knock (1985) has defined three phases of American educational philosophy: education of aristocracy, meritocratic education, and egalitarianism. As the philosophical focus shifted, new types of institutions formed and flourished. Educational opportunities of many and different kinds are now available to many citizens.

Such diversity brought new students with changed expectations of their higher education experience. The eighteen- to twenty-two-year-old male student in a residential college setting is now a minority in the total enrollment in higher education (ACE/NASPA, in press). Adult learners, minorities, and women are now represented on most college campuses. Public policy in the form of student financial aid programs has made educational opportunities available to many who would not have considered higher education an option less than half a century ago. Institutions have emerged and then evolved, to meet the educational needs of new populations seeking, sometimes demanding, access to educational opportunities.

American higher education institutions, despite their diversity, share a commitment to a unique pattern of governance. In contrast to the European system of governance by academic faculties, a corporate model of a lay board that sets policy and oversees operations is in place in American higher education. Lay governing boards, in both public and private institutions, have a controlling influence in policy development on American campuses and thus form a key constituency of the enterprise.

Student affairs, as an organizational entity, is a relatively new phenomenon in American higher education. Although many of the functions associated with student affairs have long been a part of higher education, it was not until the late 1800s that the specialty area of student affairs emerged (Fenske, 1980). Since the first dean of men and dean of women were appointed, the functions associated with student affairs grew in relation to the increased complexity of the institution and the changed needs of students. With this growth came the impetus for student affairs to cooperate, communicate, and problem solve with interested constituency groups both on and off campus.

Each institution has its own unique context. "Factors that shape the context of a particular institution include size, geographical location, funding sources, the student population, the local community, institutional traditions, internal governance systems, style of the governing board, internal political practices, and the institution's stated mission" (Barr and Keating, 1985, pp. 4-5). Within such a dynamic environment, managers need to be effective, to establish a sound foundation for the enterprise within the organization, and to commit themselves to improving their personal managerial skills.

What Is Management?

Many volumes have been written about management, and it would be impossible to reflect all that they contain in this short chapter. Gulick and Urwick (1937) developed a classical approach to management, describing the managerial functions as planning, organizing, staffing, directing, and budgeting. This approach was augmented by Weber (1947) who emphasized developing bureaucratic systems and who recognized the role that authority plays in the organization. March and Simon (1958) identified inflexibility as the major weakness in the classical approach to management. It did not account for the consequences of actions or inactions nor explain the interaction between specific acts and other actions.

Earlier, Follett (1924) developed an approach to management based on a concept of human relations. Follett postulated that the fundamental problem in organizations was the lack of a set of dynamic and harmonious working relationships within the organization. However, such a pure, human-relations approach to management ignored the formal structure of the organization. Barnard (1938) developed many of the concepts that form the basis for a behavioral approach to management. Both structural and dynamic components within organizations were identified as essential to understanding and applying management principles. Simon (1957) extended Barnard's work and postulated that an organization should be viewed as an exchange system where inducements are exchanged for work. Most of this work was done in a business setting, therefore a complete and accurate translation of these concepts to the unique environment of higher education is not always possible. Perhaps the most useful definition of management for student affairs within the context of higher education is that provided by Argyris and Schön (1974). They indicate that success in administration and management in higher education is based on the ability of the manager to develop theories of what to do in new situations and to behave humanely and effectively.

Often within the context of higher education, it is easier to define what does not work rather than what does. Walker (1979) has described the characteristics of less-effective and more-effective managers and administrators in higher education. Less-effective managers, in his view, demonstrate preoccupation with status, authority, and privilege; use of strong punitive behavior when under fire; commitment to making difficult, unpopular decisions; rule-bound behavior; and a basic conviction that subordinates and students need strong direction and control. More-effective administrators, in Walker's view, emphasize cooperation with others, coordination, open debate on the issues, acknowledgment of the legitimate interests of constituency groups, problem-solving skills, and less attention to the panoply of office. What does all of this mean for student affairs administrators? Is there a definition of management that is useful, helpful, and that can provide direction for their work?

Management: A Working Definition for Student Affairs

Transfer of traditional management concepts to student affairs is difficult. The work and products in student affairs are more diffuse than in industry, for example, and success cannot be measured by the number of items coming off the production line or by gross annual sales. A valued colleague once said that management in student affairs consists of creating an environment where good people can do good work—not a bad definition, when carefully examined, because it encompasses many of the functions of management described in traditional texts. In order to create such an environment, a student affairs manager needs to supervise, organize, delegate, coordinate, evaluate, plan, and use resources effectively.

The following working definition of management in student affairs may clarify the role and function of student affairs administration: *Management in student affairs is the process of organizing available human and fiscal resources to meet institutional and program goals in an efficient, effective, ethical, and fiscally responsible manner.* Such a definition implies skills in fiscal management (see Chapter Two), human resource management (see Chapter Three), coordination (see Chapter Four), and ethics and leadership (see Chapter Five), for management in student affairs is shaped by institutional expectations, personnel, goals, and decision-making processes.

Factors Influencing Student Affairs Management

Management, within the context of higher education, is influenced by several unique factors.

Organizational Structures. The art of management in higher education is not easily understood merely by examining a traditional organizational chart. Careful study of the organizational chart provides a perspective on the hierarchical structure of an institution; that is, who reports to whom and what subunits relate to each other. Although organizational charts in higher education may look like their corporate counterparts, the lines of authority are not as clearly drawn. This is particularly true in student affairs organizations in which a number of units usually share responsibility for the general health and welfare of students. A key to effective management within student affairs is to determine which agency is responsible for solving which problems. Otherwise, territorial questions will abound and communication problems will arise.

The overall organization of the institution experiences similar problems. Administrators, who in other settings might operate with a relatively free hand, can often move only with the tacit support of the faculty (Richman and Farmer, 1974). A number of individuals and groups, often not reflected in the formal organizational structure, must be considered and consulted in any management decision in student affairs. (See Chapter Four for a complete discussion of these issues.)

Decision Making. Management decisions are often made more complicated by the diffuse nature of the higher education enterprise. Authority, in the legal sense of the word, is easy to define. But as Richman and Farmer (1974) indicate, legal authority to act is only the tip of the organizational decision-making structure. The astute student affairs manager must be able to identify not only those individuals or groups who have legal decision-making power but also those who have the power to influence decisions. Power of this kind comes to individuals through expertise, information, political effectiveness, referent or organizational influence, judgment of others, tenure, and personal initiative (Richman and Farmer, 1974). Determining who has the power to influence decisions is a slow, but necessary, component of effective management in student affairs. Consultation, compromise, and coordination are requisite skills for student affairs managers.

Goals. Effective managers are goal directed. Not only must managers understand the goals of their specific unit or agency, they must also understand and appreciate the relationship of those goals to the institution's goals. Each college or university has a distinctive mission or purpose, and the operational goals of the institution's subunits should flow from this overall framework.

Both within and without the field of management, there has been a long-standing debate over the differences between goals and objectives. While attention to precise definitions may have value in some arenas, Deegan and Fritz (1975) use the terms interchangeably, stating that "goals or objectives describe the results we intend to accomplish, what we will have to show for the expenditure of our resources and energy" (p. 26). Johnson and Foxley (1980) describe a goal as "a desired future state. Its time frame is long-range, and it may be expressed quantitatively or qualitatively. Goals simply state where an individual, unit, or division wants to go" (p. 410). In student affairs, goal-directed management is particularly important. Higher education as a whole is characterized by ambiguous goal statements (Baldridge and Tierney, 1979); on any individual campus, understanding goals and reaching consensus about them is difficult. As long as institutional goals are "kept at an ambiguous and general level, consensus in the institution is achieved. However, as soon as goals are concretely specified and put into operation, disagreement arises" (Baldridge and Tierney, 1979, p. 21).

Student affairs divisions, agencies, and programs have a long history of ambiguous goals. Vague, general goals for student affairs have contributed to a perception that students affairs is not crucial to the academic enterprise. For example, a goal of helping students grow and develop is not useful. How will they develop? In what direction? For what purpose? Therefore, it is important that managers in student affairs set goals that give direction to programs, activities, and services. An example of such a focused goal might be to help two hundred freshmen students acquire specific skills and competencies in the area of group leadership. Such goals must be consistent with those of the institution and clearly state what will or will not be done by student affairs personnel within a specific institution. Management of the enterprise must be directed toward some end or outcome. When goals are not clear the program flounders.

Unique Management Problems in Student Affairs

Effective management of the student affairs operation is complicated by several factors.

The Organization. As previously indicated, higher education and student affairs are not line staff organizations. Usually, responsibilities are shared among several units within the students affairs organization or with other units in the university. This complicates the task of management because additional attention must be paid to communication and coordination of activities.

Disagreement on Role and Function. On many campuses, there is substantial disagreement about the appropriate role and function of student affairs. For example, should student affairs professionals be centrally involved in the development of the academic plan for the institution? Faculty and academic administrators may feel strongly that this is not the legitimate domain of student affairs, while student affairs staff may believe that their perspectives would be useful to the formulation of such a plan. When such disagreement exists, the student affairs manager must explain the unit's mission to key people within the organization.

Individual Students. Although students are the primary reason for the student affairs organization to exist, they do not easily lend themselves to management control. They will encounter problems, tragedies, and concerns that cannot be planned for in a neat management scheme. When individual students encounter problems, student affairs staff can usually help out personally. As a result, some of the more routine management tasks may not get accomplished in a timely fashion.

Student Organizations. Student organizations are not predictable. Students' behavior involving incidents such as hazing must be dealt with swiftly and promptly. Often their behavior is not negative but stems from naivety and lack of judgment. For example, they may plan an event but not follow proper procedures. Again, staff time is taken to respond and help correct potential problems.

National Issues. Volatile national issues are often reflected immediately on college campuses. Most of these issues are beyond the institution's control, but the reaction they cause on campus clearly becomes the responsibility of student affairs managers. For example, the shantytowns that sprang up on many campuses in protest of apartheid inevitably had ramifications for student affairs personnel. Policies needed to be reviewed and implemented and countless hours were spent helping both students and institutions understand the issues. When such issues arise, the routine work of management is often pushed aside in order to respond to the moment's crisis.

Outside Mandates. Any number of outside mandates have the potential to influence the effective management of student units. New federal requirements for student financial aid, as one example, required many student affairs operations to drastically change the way they processed and awarded financial aid to students. Changes in the drinking age greatly influenced operations in student activities and housing. Most units in student affairs can and will be affected by a mandate over which they have no control. And when such mandates are issued, they inevitably affect the management of the enterprise.

Legal Issues. Over the last two decades the legal environment of higher education has dramatically changed. This changed, and increasingly litigious, environment, which has had a profound influence on the management of the student affairs enterprise, has evolved from a number of factors. First, society uses legal challenges to settle differences, and colleges and universities are not immune from this trend (Van Alystene, 1968). Second, since the sixties, legal interpretations of which constitutionally protected rights must be enforced have undergone a fundamental change (Wright, 1969). Third, liability claims, particularly in the areas of alcohol, security, and safety, have grown in recent years. Claims of negligence, civil rights abuses, and discrimination are increasing (Barr, 1983). And, a new body of law is emerging that redefines the relationship between the student and the institution as contractual (Shur, 1983). Each of these developments has changed the world of work for student affairs managers. There are legal constraints on both the actions and inactions of institutional personnel. Astute practitioners become as informed as possible about the law and seek appropriate legal advice to guide their decisions.

Responsiveness. Student affairs managers, in contrast to other managers in higher education, are expected to respond immediately to problems and issues. If student behavior causes a problem, not only should that problem be confronted but methods should be developed to prevent its recurrence. There is rarely time to deliberate over alternatives; solutions must be found while the situation is in process.

Lack of Adequate Resources. Adequate human and fiscal resources are needed to provide efficient and effective student affairs programs. Lack of such resources can impede quality program development and provision of services to students (see Chapter Two for a full discussion of these issues). Other barriers to effective management in student affairs arise from the unpredictable and volatile nature of the work. Are there ways to gain control over such an enterprise? Are there methods that can be employed to reduce the amount of time and energy it takes to respond at a moment's notice? There *are* both organizational and individual actions that can help the student affairs administrator become a more effective manager.

Organizational Methods

Planning and goal setting are key skills in improving management in student affairs. Several methods appear to be particularly helpful in that process.

Develop a Student Affairs Mission Statement. Much of a manager's time is taken up with helping staff and others understand the role and function of student affairs within the institution. The development of a mission statement for the student affairs division can reduce ambiguity and increase staff effectiveness. A mission statement must be clearly linked to the institution's mission and goals. It should provide guidance to the division staff on how their work is linked to the larger educational enterprise and what goals student affairs and the institution share. For example, the role and mission statement of the division of student affairs at Texas Christian University states in part: "The Division of Student Affairs, through the departments within the Division and the Vice Chancellor, is committed to three equally important overarching goals. Each department contributes to each goal, though the activities and responsibilities of the department may cause emphasis on one specific goal. These broad goals are as follows: to provide services essential to the smooth functioning and operation of the institution, to teach students skills to manage their lives, and to provide links to enable students to integrate knowledge gained in both curricular and cocurricular settings" (Texas Christian University, 1986, pp. 1–2).

Development of a role and mission statement for student affairs takes time, energy, and commitment to the process—and the results are well worth the investment. A strong role and mission statement clearly articulates the overarching goals of the enterprise and provides a blueprint for staff work.

Develop Internal Policies. One time-consuming management task is aiding staff to decide what to do in a specific set of circumstances. Institutional policies and codes of student conduct usually provide the framework for such efforts. Staff members, however, need much more guidance to deal with unusual or tragic events. Over the past three years at Texas Christian University, we have developed internal policies to help guide our response in a number of complicated and difficult issues, such as dealing with a student death, dealing with suicide threats and attempts, and handling students who have been taking drugs or drinking. Each of the internal policy statements specifies what should be done, who should do it, and who must be involved in the ultimate resolution of the crisis. Staff members can then move forward to assume appropriate roles in managing the crisis with confidence and a feeling of support.

Supervise. One of the best uses of a manager's time is to supervise key individuals within the organization. Supervision of staff allows the manager to best utilize the human resources within the organization. (See Chapter Three for a complete discussion of supervisory issues.) Ongoing supervision also strengthens mid-management's role in the decision-making process. Mid-level managers learn the nuances of working with a manager and, through discussion, begin to understand the parameters of their role as well as their degree of freedom to take action.

Hold Staff Meetings. Regularly scheduled, well-organized staff meetings can also ease the task of management. Bringing the key actors together on a regular basis helps build a team approach to management. Questions of policy and procedure should be raised regularly with such a group. Participants' contributions strengthen the ultimate outcome and develop close working relationships. When discussion occurs regularly, many routine matters can be handled at lower levels in the organization, freeing the manager of the student affairs organization to engage in other pressing tasks.

Staff meetings are good opportunities for managers to share their perceptions of events in the larger organization; however, they should never be called merely for the sake of having a meeting. If they are well organized and if the proper issues are placed on the agenda, staff meetings can help move the organization forward.

Plan, Plan, Plan. Hanson (1980) stated that "goals provide an opportunity to state our values and philosophy more explicitly, so we must carefully consider what we hope to accomplish" (p. 277). Members of the organization must be encouraged to dream about what might be accomplished if the institution and the environment were ideal. Perhaps such ideal goals or dreams will never be realized, but articulating them provides common ground for the development of specific programs and activities. If we never take time to look into our future, it will be our present before we know it.

Broad goals will never be reached without meticulous attention to the planning process. Good planning is not a solitary activity; it involves the people who must live with any decision that is made. Each manager must develop a planning process that works in his or her setting. Whatever process is chosen, however, must be linked to a commitment that planning is important and is a priority for the organization. A serious management error is made if planning is not made a priority within the organization.

Teach. Managers in student affairs usually have a great deal of information that would be useful to others in the organization. But they rarely take the time to impart that information to others who would profit from it. An organizational commitment to teach can be met through an organized staff development program or through guided seminars on particular topics. Keeping information to oneself, unless it is confidential, is not in the manager's best interest. Programs on how the university runs, how to get things done, how to handle travel arrangements, and how to prepare payrolls are usually among the most popular staff development activities on any campus. An organizational investment in teaching staff how to function effectively within an environment pays off both in the short and long term.

Set Fiscal Guidelines. Management of fiscal resources is crucial in student affairs. Unit budget managers need to understand the institutional rules as well as what their supervisors expect of them. Using resources soundly may require shifting money from one unit to another or placing a higher priority on one activity over another. Staff members also need to understand the rules in budgeting and resource allocation and should be aided in acquiring those skills. (Chapter Two provides basic information on this important management skill.) Establishing organizational priorities and making decisions can improve managers' effectiveness.

Promote Ethical Practices. Ethical and responsible behavior should be expected within the student affairs organization. Such standards, however, are not widely understood unless there is a shared set of values within the division and unless regular discussion occurs about the ethical implications of professional practice. (See Chapter Five for a full discussion of these issues.)

Practical Methods to Improve Management Effectiveness

In addition to improving organizational practices, managers can take several specific, practical steps to improve their managerial effectiveness. Individual managers must develop their own styles and approaches to their work. There are no formulas that guarantee managerial effectiveness. The social and political climate of the workplace as well as the manager's body rhythms and personal philosophy of working with people will all influence his or her unique approach to management. There are, however, some general rules that are useful to all managers.

Rule One: Hire an Excellent Secretary or Assistant. Hiring a good secretary or assistant is one of the best decisions a manager can make. A good front-office person sets the tone for the enterprise. His or her approach to people and problems can greatly increase the effectiveness of the student affairs manager. Many problems can be appropriately redirected or solved by such an individual without intervention by the manager. The assistant must be perceptive and able to screen for problems that need the manager's attention immediately. In addition, he or she can absorb many time-consuming details, such as making travel arrangements, and free the manager for other high-priority tasks. Good support staff also do their homework and provide pertinent back-up material when information is requested or a decision needs to be made. Finally, they must be able to meet the public and represent the office in a responsible and effective manner. Care and attention must be paid during the hiring process to ensure that the manager's expectations and the candidate's qualifications closely match. Of course, the individual must be pleasant and personable, and have the needed skills for the position. Two other important attributes are the ability to make decisions and the knowledge of his or her own limitations in a specific situation.

No other single managerial responsibility is as important as employing an excellent secretary or assistant. The process can be time consuming and frustrating, but the end result is a exponential increase in the effectiveness of the manager.

Rule Two: Plan for the Unexpected. Student affairs administrators exist and work in a world that is anything but orderly. Effective student affairs managers build in time in their daily and weekly schedules to absorb the unexpected. Operationally, planning for the unexpected may have different dimensions depending on the personal style of the manager. For some, it means scheduling free time at the beginning and end of each day to respond to whatever comes up. If nothing does come up, the manager can use the time productively on other long-range activities. For other managers, it means limiting the number of meetings scheduled in a day or not having meetings or appointments scheduled back to back. For still others, planning for the unexpected means looking ahead and judging from experience which times in a semester are filled with problems—and taking steps to reduce the work load during those times. Each manager will have his or her own methods, but planning for the unexpected must be a priority in allocating a manager's time.

Rule Three: Invest Time in People. Student affairs organizations and student affairs environments are very people-intensive. Spending time with key subordinates, students, and others in the institution is time well invested. Plan time to chat informally with colleagues. Let people know when you will be available for quick drop-in visits. Schedule visits to offices and agencies within the organization. Go to student events. Managers' days should never become so filled with administrative detail that people become relegated to second-class status. Investing informal and scheduled time in people increases the manager's knowledge base and overall effectiveness. (See Chapter Four for a complete discussion of these issues.)

Rule Four: Be Clear About Expectations. Colleagues, staff members, and students will not know what a manager wants and needs unless they are told. Setting clear expectations reduces others' frustration and gives them an opportunity to let you know if what you require is impossible. Deadlines should be clear and precise and must directly relate to a legitimate need of the organization. Managers must let people know what the deadline is and why it must be met. Vague directions are very frustrating and are likely to result in an end product that is not very helpful to either the manager or the subordinate. Without delineating every nuance of a proposal or report, for example, let the individuals who are responsible know early in the process if there are special requirements in format or documentation.

Rule Five: Make a Commitment to Get Organized. The ways that a manager can get organized are myriad. Not all techniques are useful and helpful for all people. You will need to examine a variety of approaches and see what works for you. Lakein's *How to Get Control of Your Time and Your Life* (1973) provides helpful advice for managers. Lakein's suggestions for developing "to do" lists, scheduling, setting priorities, and handling paperwork have been helpful to many. Others see such approaches as nonproductive and feel trapped by the very process of getting organized. At the very least, several techniques do seem to help. First, plan beyond the present day. Get a mental picture, even if you do not write it down, of large tasks that must be accomplished in the near and far future. This aids a manager to set the direction of tasks to be accomplished. Second, take time to recap today and plan for tomorrow. Fifteen minutes spent on reflection and anticipation can make work flow more smoothly. Third, learn to deal with paperwork more efficiently and effectively.

Rule Six: Learn to Move the Paper. A typical day in any manager's office brings letters, memos, forms, announcements, and invitations. If managers do not learn how to move the paperwork, they are faced with the one task that can seem overwhelming. Some experts suggest initially sorting paperwork into priority and nonpriority items (Lakein, 1973). The easiest approach is to work through the pile, dictating responses and sending materials immediately on' to others when appropriate. Do not feel that you always have to respond formally to a memo or an inquiry. A quick note jotted at the bottom of a memo may be all that is needed. Look for ways to cut down the amount of time spent on routine paperwork. If you can do so, it will free you for more important tasks.

Rule Seven: Avoid Procrastination Whenever Possible. For most of us, there are some tasks that we just do not like to do. Therefore, we put them off until an action is absolutely necessary or until someone calls about them. Whether the task in question deals with people, paper, or policies, avoidance only exacerbates the problem and makes it even more difficult to deal with in an effective and efficient way.

Rule Eight: Learn to Delegate. Delegation is an art that is crucial to establishing the effectiveness of any manager. It is simply not possible for the manager of a complex and responsive organization to do everything. Delegation implies that you trust another person's judgment and his or her ability to resolve the problem, answer the question, or respond in an appropriate way. When tasks are delegated, give clear and specific directions. Make sure the person receiving the charge understands the deadlines involved, the action that needs to be taken, and any expectations of continued involvement.

Rule Nine: Break up Large Projects. Some tasks appear to be so large and complex that a manager will try to wait for a large block of time to get started. The large block of time rarely materializes and the task remains undone. Spend some planning time breaking large projects into smaller segments. Such planning will also help determine what information is needed to complete the task. Then proceed with the process of gathering appropriate information without waiting until the last minute. Breaking up large projects into shorter segments also gives a sense of control and direction for the task.

Rule Ten: Use a Tickle File. There are some events, issues, and concerns that do not need immediate action. Perhaps you need a response from someone else or the event is not scheduled until sometime in the future. A tickle file can help managers deal with such matters. Move the paperwork involved from your desk and note when you would like to see it again. Your secretary can then put it in a file and return it to you on the date specified. Then put it out of your mind until action needs to be taken.

Rule Eleven: Acquire the Skills You Need. All of us have skill deficits. For some, it is supervision. For others, it is budget management. For still others, it is personnel evaluation. Assess the areas that you need to improve in and then seek out assistance to meet the deficit. Classes, seminars, lectures, reading, and staff development activities can all help close the gap. With knowledge comes increased confidence that you can handle the task.

Rule Twelve: Maintain Your Sense of Humor. Keeping a perspective and a sense of humor is a necessary condition for effective management. Take time to relax and look at seemingly unsurmountable problems from a new perspective. Use humor to relieve tension. Intensive work, without any relief, is usually nonproductive. You know yourself better than anyone else and you need to pay attention to your personal needs.

Summary

Acquiring and using effective management practices within student affairs organizations is not an easy task. Principles that work in a business or an industry setting must be adapted to work in the higher education environment. The organization structure, decision-making processes, and goals of the higher education enterprise are more ambiguous than those of business and industry. A student affairs manager is not dealing with a clearly hierarchical organization. Instead, committees, expectations of others, and the overall environment must be accounted for in the work of the manager.

Skilled student affairs managers recognize the volatile and unpredictable nature of their unique environment. They must plan for the unexpected. There are methods to assist the student affairs manager to become more efficient and effective. Attention to organizational issues and personal management style can be productive and profitable. The key is for managers to build in as much predictability as possible, assess their own skills and competencies, try to overcome skill deficits, and maintain a sense of humor and perspective on their work.

References

Ambler, D. "The Administrator Role." In U. Delworth, G. R. Hanson, and Associates (eds.), *Student Services: A Handbook for the Profession.* San Francisco: Jossey-Bass, 1980.

American Council on Education and National Association of Student Personnel Administrators (ACE/NASPA). "A Perspective on Student Affairs: A Statement Issued on the Fiftieth Anniversary of *The Student Personnel Point of View.*" Washington, D.C.: American Council on Education, in press.

Argyris, C., and Schön, D. A. *Theory in Practice: Increasing Professional Effectiveness.* San Francisco: Jossey-Bass, 1974.

Baldridge, J. V., and Tierney, M. L. *New Approaches to Management: Creating Practical Systems of Management Information and Management by Objectives.* San Francisco: Jossey-Bass, 1979.

Barnard, C. I. *Functions of an Executive*. Cambridge: Harvard University Press, 1938.

Barr, M. J. "Facility Use Policies: Reducing Litigation Risks." In M. J. Barr (ed.), *Student Affairs and the Law*. New Directions for Student Services no. 22. San Francisco: Jossey-Bass, 1983.

Barr, M. J., and Keating, L. A. (eds.). *Establishing Effective Programs*. New Directions for Student Services, no. 7. San Francisco: Jossey-Bass, 1979.

Barr, M. J., and Keating, L. A. "Introduction: Elements of Program Development." In M. J. Barr, L. A. Keating, and Associates (eds.), *Developing Effective Student Services Programs: Systematic Approaches for Practitioners*. San Francisco: Jossey-Bass, 1985.

Brubacher, J. S., and Rudy, W. *Higher Education in Transition*. New York: Harper & Row, 1958.

Deegan, A. X., and Fritz, R. J. *Management by Objectives (MBO) Goes to College*. Boulder: University of Colorado, Division of Continuing Education, 1975.

Fenske, R. H. "Historical Foundations." In U. Delworth, G. R. Hanson, and Associates (eds.), *Student Services: A Handbook for the Profession*. San Francisco: Jossey-Bass, 1980.

Follett, M. P. *Creative Experience*. London: Longman's and Green, 1924.

Gulick, L., and Urwick, L. (eds.). *Papers on the Science of Administration*. New York: Institute of Public Administration, Columbia University, 1937.

Hanson, G. R. "Instruction." In U. Delworth, G. R. Hanson, and Associates (eds.), *Student Services: A Handbook for the Profession*. San Francisco: Jossey-Bass, 1980.

Johnson, C. S., and Foxley, C. H. "Devising Tools for Middle Managers." In U. Delworth, G. R. Hanson, and Associates (eds.), *Student Services: A Handbook for the Profession*. San Francisco: Jossey-Bass, 1980.

Knock, G. H. "Development of Student Services in Higher Education." In M. J. Barr, L. A. Keating, and Associates (eds.), *Developing Effective Student Services Programs: Systematic Approaches for Practitioners*. San Francisco: Jossey-Bass, 1985.

Lakein, A. *How to Get Control of Your Time and Your Life*. New York: Wyden, 1973.

March, J., and Simon, H. *Organizations*. New York: Wiley, 1958.

Richman, B. M., and Farmer, R. N. *Leadership, Goals, and Power in Higher Education: A Contingency and Open-Systems Approach to Effective Management*. San Francisco: Jossey-Bass, 1974.

Shur, G. M. "Contractual Relationships." In M. J. Barr (ed.), *Student Affairs and the Law*. New Directions for Student Services, no. 22. San Francisco: Jossey-Bass, 1983.

Simon, H. *Administrative Behavior*. (2nd ed.) New York: Macmillan, 1957.

Texas Christian University. "Role and Mission Statement of the Division of Student Affairs." Austin, Tex.: Texas Christian University, May 1986.

Van Alystene, W. A. "The Demise of the Right-Privilege Distinction in Constitutional Law." *Harvard Law Review*, 1968, *81*, 1439–1464.

Walker, D. E. *The Effective Administrator: A Practical Approach to Problem Solving, Decision Making, and Campus Leadership*. San Francisco: Jossey-Bass, 1979.

Weber, M. *The Theory of Social and Economic Organization*. New York: Free Press, 1947.

Wright, C. A. "The Constitution on the Campus." *Vanderbilt Law Review*, 1969, *22*, 1027–1088.

Fiscal management and budgeting skills are essential to sound student affairs administration.

Managing Money

Margaret J. Barr

Support for higher education has been eroding in your state. You have just returned from a meeting where a 5 percent cut in the operating budget of the university was announced. What should you do now?

Your staff has developed an exciting new student leadership program. There is no money in the budget to pay for the program. What options do you have?

The counseling center director has come to you with a proposal to expand the staff in the center by two positions. Her proposal includes charging fees for services in order to pay for the new positions. Should you support this concept?

These questions and others like them are not unusual for student affairs administrators. In fact, developing sound methods for financing programs and service is a crucial skill for student affairs administrators on the contemporary college campus.

While everyone involved in the budgeting process would agree that adequate financial support is needed, agreement on what is adequate, equitable, and fair is not easy to achieve. The debate over budgets, capital expenditures, and personnel can be difficult and is compounded by the

M. L. Upcraft and M. J. Barr (eds.). *Managing Student Affairs Effectively.*
New Directions for Student Services, no. 41. San Francisco: Jossey-Bass, Spring 1988.

changing fiscal conditions on the campuses of American colleges and universities. Resources are becoming more restricted, priorities are changing within the academic community, and all institutions are faced with increased demands for accountability and fiscal restraint from their constituent groups.

All of higher education faces these changed conditions. The problem of obtaining and maintaining adequate financial support for student affairs operations, however, has some unique dimensions. Some within the academy do not view student affairs administrators as strong fiscal managers because of decision-making errors and mounting deficits. Some administrative and faculty colleagues do not view student affairs as a central function of the institution and, consequently, student affairs operations often do not receive adequate funding. Student affairs administrators do not always clearly articulate desired program outcomes or identify the consequences of not receiving monetary support. In addition, funding for student affairs programs often relies on multiple fund sources, which creates unique problems and opportunities in fiscal management (Pembroke, 1985). Finally, student affairs administrators are generally not sophisticated in the politics and techniques of fiscal management, primarily because of limited background, experience, and training. Lack of knowledge and sophistication in an environment where resources are tight can only hinder the effort to obtain adequate resources.

This chapter is designed to help student affairs administrators broaden their understanding of both the unique and standard problems of fiscal management in their units. Specific issues will be identified, the difference between fiscal management in public and private institutions will be discussed, and methods will be identified to help student affairs administrators become better prepared to seek and hold on to their legitimate slice of the dwindling resource pie of higher education. The chapter concludes with suggestions for practice that can be adapted to any individual institutional setting.

Publics Versus Privates

Fiscal management issues differ between public and private institutions. The differences are derived from the legal organization and control of the institution, the amount of external regulation imposed on the institution, and the institution's history and tradition. Fiscal management issues within each institutional type also differ. It is therefore a mistake to assume that you understand the fiscal environment, the rules, and the obligations in any institution because of prior experience in that institutional type. You need to do your homework. Each institution or system has unique expectations for money management, and careful study is needed in order to meet them effectively.

Legal Issues. The power and authority for action, including action on fiscal matters, in public institutions is derived from the institution's statutory or constitutional entitlement. Authority for action in private institutions is derived from the institution's articles of incorporation, charter, or license. In both public and private institutions, power is vested in a governing board that is a separate entity from the individual members of the board. Any action taken, by a board member or by officers or administrators of the institution in the name of the board, must be explicitly authorized by the governing body.

Public institutions are subject to much more fiscal regulation by states than are their private counterparts. Although a few institutions in the United States are established as constitutionally autonomous, and thus are subject to less state control, most institutions in the public sector are controlled by statutes (Moos and Rourke, 1959). In addition, a public institution may be organized either as a primary agency, responding directly to the state legislature, or as a secondary agency, responding to the legislature through an intermediary agency such as a coordinating board (Alexander and Solomon, 1972). If a public college or university is part of a local or state system of higher education, it is subject to that system's rules and regulations. In some states, an institution or system reports directly to the legislature on some fiscal matters, and to an intermediary agency on others. This is the case in Illinois, where the state educational system prepares its own operating budget and defends it to the state legislature at appropriation hearings, yet must request funds for budgeted expenses through the state coordinating board.

Private institutions, in general, have greater fiscal flexibility than public institutions, but are not altogether free from state regulations. They must conform to state laws on taxes, charitable trusts, and unrelated business income. Each institution, whether public or private, develops a unique set of financial management protocols. Private and public institutions also differ in their sources of funds and their degree of legally defined autonomy.

External Regulations. External regulations influencing fiscal management come from federal, state, and private sources. Whenever outside money comes to an institution, it is accompanied by expectations and fiscal regulations. Although changes in laws, auditing requirements, and state education policies usually have little effect on private colleges and universities, these institutions are not immune to government action. If the state provides financial aid to students attending private institutions, the aid is subject to regulation and, perhaps, mandated changes in distribution, accounting, and auditing requirements. Collection and reporting of data are frequently required by financial aid programs at both the state and federal level for public and private colleges.

Public institutions must cope with mandated programs imposed by the legislature or a state agency, such as providing remedial assistance to underprepared students or ensuring access for disabled individuals to programs and services. Such mandates have enormous financial implications in terms of personnel, facilities, and program priorities if funds do not accompany the mandated program.

State and federal regulations influence how funds are allocated to program activities. For example, using appropriated funds to support auxiliary enterprises may be prohibited by state law except under certain conditions. State law may also require financial support for some functions to come from student fees. And, using student fees to support programs may be regulated as to the amount and the approval process.

In public institutions external regulations can affect personnel policies. Salary schedules may be imposed when a classification system is used for student affairs staff. Under such a system, flexibility in determining starting salaries and annual increases is diminished. Situations may also arise that make it difficult to change assignments, add staff, or fire individual nonperformers.

In both public and private colleges and universities, fringe benefits must be paid to all staff. The fringe benefit package is generally established and funded outside of the student affairs organization, although the chief student affairs officer may have substantial input in shaping it. In stable financial times, planning for fringe benefit expenses is uncomplicated. In periods of tight budgets, however, these expenses may be unilaterally transferred to the student affairs operating budget, creating a sharp decline in real funds available to meet other program needs.

Accrediting agencies, union contracts, and other external regulations and pressures can also influence the fiscal management of student affairs units. In any case, the budget is not insulated from external forces and these need to be understood in order to get things done.

Institutional Tradition. Each college or university has developed its own policies to govern fiscal affairs. Your first task as a budget manager in student affairs is to understand how to get things done in your environment. Some institutions, for example, require three outside bids on any purchase. Others require bids only on purchases over a certain dollar amount. And others do not have any bidding requirements at all. The variations are endless and purchasing is just one example of how important it is to understand local rules. As Pembroke (1985) states, "the most merited funding request imaginable will receive short shrift, however, if it is advanced in a fashion that is fundamentally inconsistent with . . . institutional funding protocols" (p. 96). He further cautions budget managers in student affairs to meet established deadlines, rarely ask for exceptions to policy, and do good staff work. His advice is well worth taking; it requires each student affairs administrator to know the rules and follow them. Even if it is not your prime responsibility, by being informed about the rules you can assist your staff, your colleagues, and your supervisor in increasing competence in fiscal matters.

Sources of Funds

All institutions depend on tuition, fees for services, grants, contracts, and endowment income to provide student services and programs. However, the amounts of money and the mix of funding sources differ among institutions. Much of the difference between public and private colleges and universities is determined by state law, which governs many financial affairs in public institutions. As a cautionary note, remember that there are also differences within each institutional type. The source of funding can influence fiscal management by imposing procedures, deadlines, and accountability. The astute fiscal manager understands these constraints and is careful to construct a budget that is not dependent on a single fund source for survival.

Budget Appropriations. Student affairs units in both public and private institutions depend on budget appropriations. In public colleges and universities, the main source of funds is the governmental body that supports the institution. Most public institutions thus depend on the appropriation process of the state legislature and governor. Some, particularly community colleges and urban institutions, are supported by a local tax base or by local governmental agencies, which can authorize the allocation of state funds.

Both public and private institutions rely on tuition revenue, but the percentage of the operating budget that is covered by tuition is significantly greater for private institutions. An additional source of the general operating budget for these is endowment income or gifts to the institution.

In both environments, the budgeting process is mandated by the sources of funds and the necessary approval processes for allocations. Public colleges and universities must meet a number of *external* deadlines, rules, and procedures. Private colleges and universities must follow a budgeting process in which *internal* regulations prevail.

Auxiliary Enterprises. Public and private colleges and universities have units that generate all or a large part of their operating budgets from sales or services. Generally, such units as residence halls, food service, student centers, health services, and athletics are classified as auxiliary enterprises. While the same budget protocols may apply for both auxiliary and appropriated budgets, auxiliary budgets require the monitoring of revenue generation and expenditures.

There are differences between public and private institutions regarding their fiscal management of auxiliary units and their procedures for deriving capital and operating budgets. In the public environment, state regulations generally mandate the fiscal management of auxiliary enterprises. Auxiliary units are expected to be self-sustaining, and all direct or indirect costs associated with them are charged back to the operation. Therefore, it is not unusual for auxiliaries at public colleges and universities to pay for all or some of the institution's utility costs, maintenance costs, student accounting operations, and other support services in business affairs. Expenditures of appropriated funds must be clearly linked to a function that serves the general educational mission of the institution. Excess income is maintained in an auxiliary reserve fund to support long-term repair, renovation, construction, or operating budget deficits. Financial reserves should be kept at a sufficient level to handle unforeseen circumstances and maintain stability in case the need arises to borrow funds for large projects.

Auxiliary enterprises in private institutions do not always operate under the strict separation rules of their public counterparts. They do not necessarily have to be self-sustaining. Income generated through such services can be viewed as part of the general income stream for the university. Usually auxiliaries receive budget support in the form of utility subsidies or absorption of other indirect costs by the institution. In turn, the auxiliaries return excess income to a general university reserve to be used as a budget-supporting mechanism for the entire institution. Under such conditions, the auxiliaries do not have exclusive use of their excess income and must compete with other units for funding for long-range renovation or capital projects (Mills and Barr, 1987).

Fees for Services. In order to meet escalating costs, public institutions in particular have begun to charge specific fees for certain services. Counseling centers and health services, for example, have gained partial support of their operating budgets by charging fees for certain clinical services. Such an approach is based on a philosophy that those who directly use the services should pay the cost.

When charging fees for services, a number of secondary questions must be answered. What services should be free? What services should have a fee attached? What rates will you charge? For example, in an institution with a mandatory student health insurance program, fees may be directly linked to the insurance benefits available to students. Careful attention must be paid to these questions and others unique to the institutional environment when developing a policy to charge fees for certain services. It is an approach that has both problems and opportunities for the budget manager and should only be used in very specific circumstances consistent with the educational philosophy of the institution.

Student Fees. Funding for student affairs units in both public and private institutions is heavily dependent on student fees. Differences arise between public and private institutions not only in the processes of setting the fees but also in the allocation of such fees. Public colleges and universities may have to adhere to legislative limits on fees and be constrained in the application of certain fees to certain units. In addition, setting and distributing fees is usually a complex and very open process. Students are often highly involved in fee allocation committees and decisions are never final until a vote is taken. In the public environment, the student affairs administrator must provide information about the current budget and requests for increases as well as historical information to aid committee members in understanding the implications of their decisions.

In addition to procedural questions, there are legal and policy questions to be considered when setting student fees. Is it possible to use student activity fees to support such programs as a birth control information service that may be considered controversial by part of the academy? Should and can the institution adopt a fee package that includes both mandatory and optional fees? These are complex questions and must be given careful attention if student fees are an important revenue source for student affairs operations.

In the private sector, establishment and distribution of fees is usually considered an administrative matter. Fees are a part of the institution's overall fiscal plan and can usually be reallocated to meet new needs. Justification of requests for funds is certainly needed, but the process at private institutions is less externally political and public. Fees are an important source of income for student affairs programs in both institutional types. And approval for a change in fees in any setting must be sought from the governing board.

Grants. Federal and state grants are another source of revenue for student affairs programs. Relying on them, however, is risky. When grant funds are awarded, it is usually expected that the institution will eventually absorb the costs of the program into its own operating budget. Administrators must be careful not to raise expectations on campus for the continuation of programs if there is not a long-term grant commitment. Federal and state grants can be a powerful source of supplemental funding for current programs, or they can provide the opportunity to prove the viability of experimental programs. Be sure, in any case, that you and your administrative superior understand and are able to meet the obligations attached to such funds.

Other Sources. There are a number of other fund sources that can support student affairs programs and services, including income from facility rental to outside groups, leasing arrangements with outside vendors, vending machine contracts, damage fees, fines, and so on. Although each of these income sources is in itself slight, in combination they can provide significant income for student affairs programs and should be accounted for realistically in the budgeting process.

Recommendations. Each type of funding support has inherent risks and rewards for the student affairs budget manager.

1. *Do not rely on only one source of funds for a program if you have a choice.* Depending on only one source of funds for a program unit is usually a mistake. Under such conditions, the program unit is vulnerable to sudden disruption of support if its single fund source is withdrawn.

2. *The decision to charge fees for services should be very carefully evaluated.* Some approaches to funding, such as user fees, have ethical implications. For example, those that need the services the most may not be able to use them if fees are charged.

3. *General budget funds should play a significant part in student affairs budgeting.* When funds from the general budget are provided to student affairs, there is a clear link between student affairs and the prime academic mission of the institution. Although a mixed-fund approach to budgeting creates complications in student affairs budgeting, the advantages far outweigh the disadvantages. As Mayhew (1979, p. 54) says, "budgets are really statements of educational purpose phrased in fiscal terms." If student affairs programs are relegated to pay-as-you-go operations, then they are clearly not central to the operation of the institution.

4. *Look at the long-term implications of funding decisions.* Each college or university will develop and implement funding patterns that make sense in its environment. Careful thought must be given, however, to any radical shift in funding of student affairs that may be proposed to meet short-term resource problems. Decisions made today will influence the quality of student affairs programs and their centrality or marginality within the institution for decades to come.

Operating budgets are only one source of concern for student affairs. The way in which major renovations and new facility construction costs are managed within the institution must also be studied. Capital budgeting plans and programs are essential elements in strong student affairs programs.

Capital Budgeting

Construction of new facilities and renovation of existing facilities present some of the most complicated fiscal problems in higher education. Deferred maintenance is a problem looming for every college or university in the United States (National Association of College and University Business Officers, 1984). Approaches to funding such undertakings differ markedly between and among private and public colleges and universities. Decisions on capital budgeting are usually driven by the institution's philosophy on long-term debt, the current state of physical facilities, and the history of the institution. Whether the institution is private or public, large or small, understanding how capital expenditures are approached within the environment is essential. Five major approaches exist for funding capital expenditures: self-financing, loans, bonds, gifts, and joint enterprises with the community or business and industry. Each method has long-term and short-term budget implications. The method chosen will be determined by the financial philosophy of the institution, the legal parameters on fiscal affairs, and the current realities facing decision makers.

Self-Financing. Under the self-financing approach, the institution borrows money from itself to finance large expenditures. The loan is amortized over a set period of time and is paid back from the operating budget. Many institutions establish a repair and renovation account and fund it by allocations from the annual operating budget. This approach limits the amount of money that can be expended in any one year to the availability of reserve funds and usually is not appropriate for major construction projects.

Another self-financing approach is to borrow from the endowment of the institution and repay the amount borrowed from the operating budget over a set period of time. The disadvantage that endowment income is reduced over the period of the loan can be offset by including an obligation to repay both the principal and the projected loss of income from the endowment funds in the amortization plan.

A final alternative relies on careful fiscal planning. When a new facility is constructed, an endowment specific to that facility is established to handle repair, renovation, and operating costs associated with the building. The use of repair and renovation accounts is used extensively in both public and private institutions. Borrowing from an institution-wide endowment is usually a limited option in public institutions but has been used successfully as a financial strategy in private colleges and universities. Endowment of facilities at the time of construction is clearly the best alternative for both institutional types, but does not provide a method to handle the long-term deferred maintenance costs facing unendowed facilities. However, endowment of specific facilities may not be an option in public colleges and universities due to fiscal constraints imposed by state regulations.

Loans. In the sixties and seventies the federal government provided a number of low-cost loan programs to enhance facility construction in higher education. Although such programs have diminished in recent years, they are still available for certain projects in campus housing, science facilities, and libraries. They have the advantage of low interest rates and long amortization periods that spread the cost to the operating budget over decades. Despite the obvious advantages, such approaches to capital funding may be in conflict with the financial philosophy of the institution. Care should be exercised in meeting funding needs by mortgaging the future to pay for the past. Furthermore, the problem of deferred maintenance still must be confronted.

Private lending institutions also have made funds available to colleges and universities for construction and renovation projects. The same problems occur as with government loans, and there is the added disadvantage of higher interest rates. However, restrictions on use of funds can be directly negotiated with the lender, and less governmental regulation prevails.

Bonds. Bonds have become the most popular form of financing facility construction in public institutions. Although few private colleges and universities have entered the bond market, the trend is growing. Thus, understanding the implications of bonding as an approach to financing institution facilities is essential. Bonds are sold by the institution on the open market to finance projected debt, and future revenue such as user fees, student fees, and dormitory or facility rental income is pledged to pay back the bonds and interest. Disclosure requirements often make this alternative unattractive to private institutions, since in order for an institution to float bonds, a service such as Standard and Poors or Moody must provide a credit rating. The resulting outside scrutiny can have public relations and fiscal implications for the institution.

During the late seventies and early eighties, there was a strong trend in many institutions to consolidate long-term debts by issuing new bonds. Some institutions arbitraged funds obtained from bond sales and used the revenue to meet pressing short-term fiscal needs. New federal regulations make this approach much less attractive in today's market. As with other long-term financing plans, bonds have the disadvantage of indebting the institution well into the future to pay for past projects.

Gifts. A gift that pays the entire cost of building or renovating a facility is obviously the best approach to capital expenditures. It is not without problems, however. Receiving gift support requires locating potential donors, and in this economy that is not always easy. Moreover, some donors feel that they should have control of the project, including such details as the choice of decorator or contractor. Under most circumstances, these problems can be avoided by involving key decision makers from the onset in the funds acquisitions process. Private institutions have a long history of receiving gift support for major capital expenditures, but this source has been relatively untapped in the public sector. New tax laws make this alternative less attractive, but when it does occur, many long-term capital problems are resolved.

Joint Enterprises. On many campuses, a new approach to capital funding is emerging. Institutions enter into joint ventures with business, industry, or local government to fund either facilities or programs. Usually this approach occurs when both parties benefit and when the project meets a central educational need of the college or university. Often the institution donates land, provides planning support, and commits resources to the long-term operation of the venture. The private sector provides the capital for construction and start-up operating costs. Although this approach to capital expenditures has the advantage of expediency, it does have problems that must be avoided. Joint enterprises must be carefully negotiated to protect the academic domain from unwarranted pressure and outside influence. Control of the facility and what goes on there must be explicitly understood in order for the educational philosophy of the institution to prevail.

Summary. Whatever approach to long-term capital budgeting the institution takes, student affairs administrators must understand it well in order to get new facilities and maintain current operations. With fiscal resources becoming more restricted, innovative approaches are needed to finance capital expenditures on many campuses. A well-informed student affairs manager who can ask the right questions becomes a key player in getting appropriate capital expenditures made in student affairs.

Financial Strategies for New Programs

When resources are tight, new programs are not looked upon favorably unless they can be directly linked to improvements in the educational environment. The first question to ask is, Can the new program be funded by the reallocation of existing resources? By not addressing this question, student affairs managers may miss an opportunity for funding new programs. Managers should inquire whether new programs can be implemented with current resources by reallocating funds or by dropping long-time program efforts that are no longer successful. For example, a new vice-chancellor for student affairs inherited a situation in which computer funds and support for units were woefully lacking. Rather than going to the chancellor and asking for new funds to support the computerization effort, she carefully reviewed all the budgets within the division. By placing new budget protocols into effect, she was able to pool funds from several existing units to fund computerization of key units within the division. The key to success was the involvement of all unit heads in the decision-making process. If they could see that giving up something now enabled another unit to advance, *and* they knew that their priorities were also being considered in an overall plan, they could be supportive.

Over a three-year period of fund consolidation, five units received at least minimal computer support, and a long-term strategy was in place to provide needed software and hardware for other units in the division. By first looking within to accomplish a needed priority, the student affairs division established a precedent of internal reallocation.

When a new program priority in the area of drug and alcohol education later emerged the proposal for funds was taken seriously; in other words it was not assumed that student affairs was just asking for more money without exercising fiscal constraint. Societal pressures to deal with the issue of substance abuse were mounting, and the timing was correct. The new proposal contained a carefully designed program statement explicitly outlining what would and would not happen as the result of the influx of new funds. The proposal was modest and, because of the track record established in student affairs, it was not picked apart line by line. The vice-chancellor was clear about what was needed, what was wanted, and what the minimal funding requirements were in order to make a difference.

Timing of new program proposals is crucial. Student affairs professionals need to adhere to budgetary guidelines and be prepared to present the new program request when it logically fits into the decision-making process. Several rules are important in making requests for additional or new funding.

1. *Know what you want.* Be prepared to clearly and succinctly state what will or will not happen if the funding request is denied.

2. *Know what you can live with.* Budgeting is an art requiring compromise, negotiation, and problem resolution. You must understand what the minimum requirements are to provide a quality program. If it is simply not possible to provide the program under the fiscal constraints imposed by the institution, do not take the money. Wait and go back to the table another day.

3. *Do not surprise other decision makers.* It is usually useful to discuss problems with others involved in the budgeting process and to try to engage them in solving the problems. People are more apt to support what they helped create.

4. *Involve your administrative superior.* Spending a great deal of time and effort on a funding proposal that does not have the support of your administrative superiors is a waste of time and effort. Find out what they can and will support, then develop strategies to involve them in budget and request preparation.

5. *Be willing to give up something.* Higher education is past the phase of unlimited expansion. In order to meet new priorities, we may have to give something up. When it is a favorite program or activity, the choice may be difficult. The key is to remember what outcomes you are seeking and how a new program effort can advance them.

6. *Be honest.* Be precise in your program requests for financial support. Do not submit requests asking for more than you want with the hope that after cuts are made you will end up with what you need. Such strategies merely reinforce the notion that student affairs administrators are not careful stewards of resources.

New funds are obtainable only if you do your homework, develop justifiable proposals, and are willing to take a strong stand about what can be accomplished within the fiscal constraints of the institution.

The Internal Budget Process

Building a budget request for a student affairs division requires hard work and attention to detail. Budget protocols within a division must conform to general institutional rules while still allowing for flexibility. One method that has achieved some degree of popularity is a zero-based budget approach. Under such a system, each unit builds its budget requests from scratch, justifying each expenditure in terms of goals and program outcomes. A zero-based budget approach gives the overall budget manager clear informaton on priorities and links the final budgeting process to program goals. Zero-based budgeting is, however, a time-consuming and often frustrating process for unit budget managers.

Another approach is for the chief student affairs officer to provide units with the same level of funding as the previous year while setting aside a central pool of additional funds for new and pressing priorities. Unit budget managers must justify requests for additional funds first by demonstrating that these priorities cannot be met with existing resources and then by competing for new funds with one another.

A third approach is to pool all money centrally, including incremental funds, for certain line items such as equipment. This permits the overall budget manager to move money around from unit to unit in order to meet pressing one-time needs. Again, access to the central fund pool must be justified by program proposals.

Whatever approach is chosen, the following suggestions should aid in developing a reasonable approach to internal budgeting.

1. *Develop clear rules.* Make sure that all unit budget managers understand the rules. Be available to assist them, particularly if procedures have changed from the previous year.

2. *Ask people what they need.* Although you may not be able to meet all funding requests, it is important to ask budget managers what they need. Formula budgeting of any kind never allows units to express their concerns about long-standing budget deficiencies.

3. *Talk to budget managers about their requests.* As you are making final budget decisions, provide an opportunity to talk face to face with affected budget managers. They will feel that at least you care enough to listen even if you cannot fund their request.

4. *Explain your decisions.* Preparing budget requests is hard work and budget managers deserve an answer to their requests. Provide information that helps them understand, even if they cannot agree with, your decision.

34

Suggestions for Practice

Budgeting and sound fiscal management are key skills in higher education administration and in the sub-specialty of student affairs. Although academic administrators may be equally unskilled fiscal managers as student affairs administrators, they are traditionally more protected in the budget allocation process. Thus, funding and budgeting skills become even more crucial for student affairs administrators. In this era of tight resources, there are more declarations that student services are not essential and that direct institutional support for such enterprises needs to be diminished (Chait, 1982). Adherence to a few simple rules can help the student affairs manager get and keep the necessary resources to provide quality programs.

1. *Understand the rules.* This requires doing homework, talking to people, not making assumptions, and adhering to guidelines. Investing time and effort in understanding the institutional context can pay off when serious budget negotiations are necessary.

2. *Follow the rules.* This sounds almost too simple to be a guideline, but it can provide the most solutions for student affairs management. Because student affairs administrators have historically not been fully involved in fiscal management, we often are not as aware as we should be of the rules and thus get into difficulty. Following the rules also establishes your credibility as a fund manager.

3. *Ask for help.* Often you will encounter problems in fiscal management and budgeting. If you made a mistake, own up to it and try to get it resolved. If you are encountering a problem for the first time, ask someone in fiscal affairs to help you design a strategy to deal with it. You can learn something in the process and gain credibility at the same time.

4. *Have a plan.* Most fiscal questions in student affairs can be handled efficiently if you have a plan. This requires developing alternate proposals and involving others in the planning process to ensure that you are making the best decisions based on the best available information.

5. *Look for long-term consequences.* Since funding in student affairs often relies on multiple fund sources, it is essential that you understand the long-term consequences of changes in sources of support or implementation of new fees or costs. Look into the future and be prepared to support your assumptions about consequences with experience, data, and facts. A short-term solution to a funding problem may have long-term negative consequences for the program.

6. *Keep track of expenditures.* Again this may be a rule that is so simple that it need not be stated. However, the credibility of student affairs operations can be compromised if there are budget overruns. Careful attention to expenditures can help you identify trends and problems before they are insurmountable. You may be able to cut back on

expenses or, at a minimum, warn others of escalating cost overruns that are beyond your control.

7. *Devise multiple-year approaches.* Often a pressing facility or equipment need cannot be funded during one fiscal year. Look for methods to break the project up into segments that, added together over several fiscal years, can meet the goal. Such a strategy, however, mandates careful planning and agreement among all parties.

8. *Link your efforts.* Too often, student affairs budgets and budget requests are mistakenly treated as stand-alone activities. Successful long-term fiscal support for student affairs can only be obtained if the activity or program is directly linked to the mission of the institution. If that essential linkage is missing, student affairs programs can easily be characterized as peripheral and funded accordingly.

9. *Build consortiums.* Often there are others in the institution interested in the same program and activity. Funding can then be easily achieved, with many units contributing to the same program or sharing certain equipment or services across budgetary lines. Failure to identify possible consortium approaches to funding often results in duplicate expenditures within the institution and loss of available income to meet other pressing needs. Computerization provides many such opportunities for consortium approaches, in which software can be used by more than one department without loss in efficiency to any.

10. *Exercise constraint.* Always be on the lookout for less expensive and more effective ways to conduct business. Even if these alternatives are not adopted, they will demonstrate the student affairs division's commitment to fiscal accountability and restraint.

11. *Make suggestions.* Just because something has always been done in the same way does not mean it is the best approach. At many institutions the old saying, "there is a right way, a wrong way, and the XYZ way," is the norm. Nonetheless, be respectful when suggesting change because there may indeed be reasons unknown to you for certain approaches.

12. *Understand implications.* Personnel costs are usually the least understood in student affairs. Undoubtedly, we understand the actual costs charged to our budgets for a new position, but there are hidden institutional costs which must also be absorbed. Know the real cost of what you propose even if it is not coming directly out of your budget allocation. Preparation on such details again demonstrates your understanding of the entire institutional picture.

13. *Own up to your mistakes.* We all make mistakes. Unfortunately, sometimes we try to cover them up or pretend that they do not exist. This is a mistake in all aspects of administration but even more of a problem in fiscal matters. If you have erred, seek help in correcting it and learn how not to do it again.

14. *Be accountable.* Although the institution may have a number of protocols in fiscal management, they are usually not sufficient for sound student affairs operations. Because our work is so people-intensive and outcomes are difficult to measure, we are required to develop additional mechanisms for assessing outcomes.

15. *Use multiple fund sources.* Because student affairs budgets are usually supported by multiple fund sources, they are less subject to changes in funding circumstances. Using multiple fund sources also gives the budget manager increased flexibility to deal with new ideas, new priorities, and new programs.

Conclusions

At the beginning of this chapter, several questions were posed that a student affairs manager may routinely encounter. The answers to those questions depend on a number of factors, including internal budgetng protocols, institutional tradition, and the sources of funds used to support the program request. An effective budget manager in student affairs understands institutional expectations and consistently follows established guidelines. Both short-term and long-term implications must be considered in any fiscal decision. A short-term solution may only create larger and more difficult funding questions in the future.

Capital budgets require special attention and analysis. Decisions regarding capital projects may influence the availability of resources to fund ongoing programs and services. Furthermore, the sources of funds to support student services programs must be carefully considered. Each source has advantages and disadvantages. However, it is essential not to relegate the student affairs program to a pay-as-you-go operation. When student affairs programs are not supported by institutional funds, the centrality of student affairs services in the institution is not recognized.

Finally, acquiring fiscal management skills takes time and patience. Relatively simple approaches seem to work best, and a number of suggestions for practice are included in this chapter. It is crucial that you maintain an attitude open to learning and asking questions, and not make assumptions. If you pay attention to acquiring and using sound fiscal management skills, you can gain great credibility in the process and usually succeed in capturing adequate resources for the student affairs enterprise.

References

Alexander, K., and Solomon, E. *College and University Law.* Charlottesville, Va.: Mickie, 1972.

Chait, R. P. "An Obituary for Student Affairs: Is There Life After Death?" Paper presented at the National Association of Student Personnel Administrators, Boston, April 1982.

Mayhew, L. B. *Surviving the Eighties: Strategies and Procedures for Solving Fiscal and Enrollment Problems*. San Francisco: Jossey-Bass, 1979.

Mills, D., and Barr, M. "Private vs. Public Institutions: How Do Financial Issues Compare?" Washington, D.C.: AACD Press, 1987.

Moos, M., and Rourke, F. *The Campus and the State*. Baltimore, Md.: Johns Hopkins Press, 1959.

National Association of College and University Business Officers. "NACUBO Prepares Comparative Financial Data on Revenues and Expenditures." *Business Officer*, 1984, *17* (7), 6-7.

Pembroke, W. J. "Fiscal Constraints on Program Development." In M. J. Barr, L. A. Keating, and Associates (eds.), *Developing Effective Student Services Programs: Systematic Approaches for Practitioners*. San Francisco: Jossey-Bass, 1985.

Managing staff for high productivity and high morale means recruiting, selecting, training, supervising, and evaluating them effectively.

Managing Staff

M. Lee Upcraft

The final three candidates for a counseling position in your counseling center all have glowing recommendations and they finished in a dead heat in the interviews. Whom do you select?

You have received the usual requests from your staff for funds to attend yearly national professional conferences and, as usual, you do not have enough money to send them all at full reimbursement. What do you do?

You have just been appointed the director of student activities in a unit consisting of very experienced people with very low morale. How do you handle this situation?

One of your staff is not at all pleased with your yearly job performance evaluation. She believes she is a very high-performing staff member, while you believe she is marginal at best. How do you proceed?

These and other supervisory dilemmas are often perplexing, even to the most experienced manager. In Chapter One, Margaret Barr began her definition of management with these words: "the process of organizing available human . . . resources." In other words, management starts with

M. L. Upcraft and M. J. Barr (eds.). *Managing Student Affairs Effectively.*
New Directions for Student Services, no. 41. San Francisco: Jossey-Bass, Spring 1988.

people, and managing them in a way that produces results is critical to a manager's success and the success of the student affairs enterprise.

Getting the job done for students and the institution requires maintaining high staff productivity and high staff morale, and there is abundant evidence in business management literature to support this contention. Blake and Mouton (1964) identify two dimensions of effective leadership as concern for production and concern for people. Hersey and Blanchard (1977) label these dimensions task orientation and relationship orientation. And there is evidence (Burke, 1980) that task and relationships are of equal importance, regardless of the situation.

This chapter explores the problems of student affairs managers in maintaining high productivity and high morale. Managing staff is a four-step process that begins with recruiting and selecting the right people for the right job. Orienting and training these people is the second step. The third and most important step is providing supervision that encourages high productivity and high morale. The final step is measuring productivity and morale through performance evaluations.

The Problems of Balancing High Productivity and High Morale

Many student affairs managers, by instinct or formal training, are not comfortable balancing high productivity and high morale. Those of us educated as student development specialists or as counselors tend to put the individual first. Serving the best interests of the individual, above all else, is our goal. Many student affairs managers tend to manage their staff by putting the interests of individual staff members ahead of meeting responsibilities to students and the institution.

The organizational setting conspires to enhance such instincts. Our staffs interact more with us than with students, they are more assertive and mature than most students, and they know how to manipulate organizations, in part for their own benefit. Neither bosses nor staffs intend to put themselves ahead of students or the institution, but often that is exactly what happens. The worst outcome is that student affairs managers lack the courage to confront inappropriate behavior or low performance for fear of hurting staff feelings or endangering the supervisor-subordinate relationship.

On the other hand, institutional priorities and tasks may assume such importance that staff morale is ignored or damaged. For example, an institution can make unrealistic demands on too few staff. The message to these overworked staff members is clear: The institutions cares much more about getting the job done that it does about the people doing it. This may be especially true in institutions where student affairs is undervalued or unappreciated.

Recruiting and selecting the right people can be difficult. Because there are many different routes to the profession, through formal training or job experience, formal credentialing is absent as a means of screening and selecting staff. Consequently, we rely on the interpersonal impressions created in the interview process and references (which when written are almost totally useless) and then select the best who apply. Also, our profession is very diverse, consisting of managers, administrators, counselors, student development specialists, and others; thus different criteria are used when hiring for different jobs.

Resources to enhance staff morale may be deficient. The salaries of student affairs staff may be less than faculty or other staff. It is hard to encourage high staff morale if staff perceive they are paid less for doing more important jobs or that they work longer hours than their institutional colleagues. Also, resources for staff development and training may be the first to be cut in budget reductions. Unfortunately, we have not been very creative in developing nonmonetary rewards for high-performing staff.

Finally, in student services the evidence of staff productivity is often "soft" and not easily measured. Although "hard" evidence, such as student academic achievement and retention, may be appropriate for measuring organizational effectiveness, it is almost never used to evaluate staff performance. So we measure performance on impressions, subjective criteria, and outright prejudice—or we do not measure performance at all. Or we may measure performance on an employee's relationship to the boss or the organization, without regard to productivity.

Managing staff in student affairs is not easy, but it is not impossible. The following sections offer practical suggestions for managing staff to produce desired results and high morale.

Step 1: Recruit and Select the Right People

Putting square pegs in round holes is always a mistake. As one wag put it, "Never try to teach a pig to sing; it wastes your time and it annoys the pig." Selecting the right people for the right job is easier said than done, but it is well worth the effort. As noted earlier, formal credentials are not much help, and diversity within the profession complicates the situation. So what can be done?

Know What the Job Is. It is the rare person who has looked at his or her formal job description and concluded that it accurately represents what he or she actually does. Job descriptions should be rewritten when vacancies occur and should be based on the needs of the organization. But people in the organization must agree on what the job is and communicate the job requirements in a consistent manner to candidates. Once the position is filled, the job description should be reviewed periodically to make sure that what the person does is what is in the job description.

Know What You Are Looking For. In addition to the formal education and relevant experience, skills, and knowledge required for the position, there should be extensive discussion of what kind of person you are looking for. Certain jobs and organizations need certain types of people to fulfill the goals. Everyone involved in the selection process should discuss and agree on professional skills and personality characteristics as well as formal credentials.

Act Affirmatively. Very few student affairs organizations have satisfied their commitment to hiring women, ethnic minorities, the disabled, and other categories of persons who are legally protected from discrimination. Even if women and minorities are in the organization, they are often in the lower levels. Acting affirmatively means expanding deficient internal candidate pools by regional or national searches and hiring qualified minorities and women when their qualifications exceed or are equal to those of other candidates.

Check References. Recently, because of the right of candidates to know what is written about them in letters of recommendation, written recommendations are virtually useless because they seldom contain negative comments. But personal or telephone reference checks are vital and useful. However, when expanded beyond the candidate's listed references, these checks should be done only with the approval of the candidate. The candidate's current supervisor is an especially important reference. Secondary references (asking a candidate's reference to give you the name of another person who could comment on the candidate's qualifications) can be useful but may be risky if the candidate does not wish others to know of his or her candidacy.

Develop a Screening Process That Is Clear to Everyone. Decide who is screening and why. Generally speaking, all levels of the organization should be represented, and persons outside the organization with a vested interest should be represented. If a search committee is used, its task should be clearly defined before it begins. Search committees can screen, recommend, prioritize, or actually decide on candidates. Whatever the model, the role of the search committee should be clear, and, as a general rule, managers should make the final decision based on information presented by the search committee.

Determine the Scope of the Search. Decide whether you think you can fill the position internally or if a regional or national search is required. Generally speaking, regional or national searches for all positions are recommended as a means to ensure the best possible candidate pool and that women and minorities are adequately represented. Internal candidates are sometimes threatened by a national search, but if they are qualified, they will compete successfully.

Make Sure Candidates Are Fully Informed. Prior to the interview, candidates should know the institution, organization, community, job, criteria for hiring, hiring process, and who makes the final decision.

Develop an Interview Plan. Everyone involved in the interview process should know and understand it. It goes without saying that all candidates should be treated the same, although this does not always happen. Interviewers should review the questions to be asked and discuss desired answers. Job-related scenarios can be used to allow candidates to demonstrate judgment. Presentations on relevant topics can demonstrate knowledge and group presentations skills. Ample time for candidates' questions should be allowed. In fact, the quality of a candidate's questions, or the lack of any questions at all, can provide interviewers with additional data about the candidate.

Share Information and Decide. Each candidate should be discussed and a prioritized list of acceptable candidates developed for the person making the final decision. At this point, other organizational commitments, such as affirmative action goals, should be considered. If the list of acceptable candidates does not include women and minorities, the person making the final decision should make sure that a real effort was made to recruit and screen affirmatively. It is also very legitimate for the final decision maker to review women and minorities considered but not recommended.

Offer, Negotiate the Contract, and Hire. Sometimes managers have wide latitude in negotiating salary, benefits, job responsibilities, and working conditions, and sometimes they do not. Persons offered positions should know what is negotiable—and what is not—and the range of possibilities within what is negotiable.

Inform Unsuccessful Candidates as Soon as Possible. When the successful candidate has accepted the position, unsuccessful candidates should be informed in advance of a public announcement and given feedback if they request such information.

Step 2: Orient and Train the Right People

Develop an Orientation Plan. The supervisor should take direct responsibility for helping a new employee get oriented to the new job and should present a plan, on the first day of work, based on the principles listed below. The new employee should be given a chance to revise that plan to meet his or her needs.

Help Staff Get to Know Key People in the Organization. It is important for a new employee to get to know the important people, in the organization and in the institution, that will make the employee more effective. Supervisors should take the initiative in setting up "getting acquainted" appointments with these people and actually accompany new employees to these appointments.

Help New Staff Learn About the Organization. New staff must learn about informal organizational dynamics. Who do you need to have on your side if you want to promote an idea? What is the boss really like, and how can he or she be "managed?" How can you really get into trouble in this organization? How do you find out what is really going on? Colleagues are the best resource for answering these questions, and supervisors should ensure that colleagues are available to help new staff members.

Build in Extensive Supervisor Time. Formal, weekly meetings between the supervisor and the new staff member—and other meetings as needed—are strongly recommended. The orientation plan can be reviewed and revised to meet emerging needs of the organization and the new employee.

Assign a Senior Staff Colleague to "Mentor." Colleagues can be very helpful to new employees, but when everyone has responsibility, sometimes no one gets the job done. So new employees should have a colleague assigned to "mentor" their orientation and help them produce results.

Do a Three-Month Performance Evaluation. New employees need to know early on how they are doing. Supervisors should conduct a formal three-month performance evaluation to identify progress to date, strengths, and areas of growth. If the new employee is a poor performer, the supervisor must take immediate steps to promote improvement. Overlooking a poor start may well create future problems if improvement is lacking.

Establish Organizational Commitment to Training. Too often, lip service is given to training but time and resources do not follow. Supervisors must allow time for staff to participate in training and allocate resources to make it happen. In times of lean budgets, other things than training should be cut.

Know What You Are Training For. In general, organizations train to increase knowledge, develop skills, or increase awareness. Training should be designed to address these three components, and it should be clear what the training is designed to do. For example, the recent AIDS epidemic probably requires training that includes more knowledge about the disease, more skill in dealing with AIDS victims, and greater awareness of the social and cultural implications of the disease.

Train for the Organization First. Train for what the organization must accomplish through its individuals. The purpose of training is to help staff do the best job possible within the mission and goals of the organization. Training should be directly related to the knowledge, skills, and awareness required to get the job done. Training for the individual should be a second priority, when consistent with organizational goals and the individual's professional development and career path.

Plan for Training. Too often, it is left to the employee to choose which conventions to attend. Training goals of the organization should be developed and then implemented through a training plan for each individual. When this is done, it may be discovered than an onsite training workshop is more cost effective and can be tailored to meet local needs. You may also find that topic-oriented workshops may be more suited to training than general purpose, national, professional conventions.

Use Experienced Trainers. While persons within the organization can frequently train other staff, in general, it is better to use persons outside the organization for training. Outsiders do not have vested interests in the outcomes of the training and may have a more objective picture of what needs to be done and how to do it.

Evaluate Training. Training should be evaluated on the basis of staff satisfaction with the training efforts. It should also be evaluated on the basis of intended eventual outcomes. For example, if a goal of the counseling center is to do more and higher-quality short-term therapy, did the training actually make a difference in meeting this goal?

Step 3: Supervise for Productivity and Morale

Although high productivity and high morale must be equally balanced in effective management, it is also important to tailor supervision to the organization and the individuals in it. Supervision may be close and structured or highly delegatory. Some staff will function best within structure, while others will function best with a high degree of autonomy. New staff may require closer supervision than experienced staff. And some jobs, by their nature, require closer supervision than others.

Likewise, some organizations function in a more structured way than others. In academic administration, for example, faculty function with a high degree of autonomy and very little supervision, particularly after tenure has been achieved. Some student services, such as student aid, function within highly structured federal and state regulations, and thus closer supervision may be required.

But there are some supervisory principles that cut across individual and organizational differences and needs. Supervisors are more likely to produce results with high morale if they follow some commonsense guidelines.

Clearly Communicate Your Leadership Style. Everyone in your organization should know your style and be able to predict your behavior with some accuracy. That, of course, assumes you know your style and are consistent in your leadership. There may even be some merit in putting your leadership philosophy and style in writing for all to see.

Care a Lot. The best supervisors are those that really care. They care a lot about getting the job done and about the people working for them. These managers are honest, fair, predictable, courageous, maintain confidences, and have integrity. (The importance of these characteristics are discussed further in Chapter Five.)

Establish Clear Goals for Staff. Staff have a right to know what is expected of them. It is the responsibility of the supervisor to establish goals in consultation with staff members. The results expected should be clearly defined in writing, and timetables for producing them should be established.

Insist on Frequent Communication. Even if the boss is a close supervisor, there should be a time each week when the boss and each staff member sit down and discuss issues, problems, goals, progress on tasks, and anything else central to productivity and morale. There should be a weekly meeting even if there seems to be no reason for meeting, because the contact is important and because there are always issues to be discussed.

Manage Positively. Henry Kissinger supposedly once defined praise as those moments of silence between criticisms. However, all things considered, the carrot works better than the stick. Supervisors should reinforce positive behavior and productivity frequently and in highly visible ways. Too often, we call attention to mistakes, not to results. It should be clear that when results are produced, everyone will know. A positive reinforcement leadership style produces results and morale.

Insist on Accountability. The "stick," however, also works and is sometimes necessary. Managing positively does not mean that mistakes are ignored or that poor performance is tolerated. Staff should know that failure to produce will be recognized and steps taken to ensure results the next time. This means that the manager not only helps staff improve their skills but occasionally punishes them as well. Verbal reprimands in private are perfectly appropriate if accompanied by a strategy for improvement. The ultimate punishment is, of course, firing the staff member who consistently fails to produce results.

Decide Who Decides and Why. Every supervisor operates within organizational constraints. Staff need to know when you are operating within nonnegotiable institutional policies and decisions. However, every supervisor also has freedom to operate within his or her scope of responsibility. Staff should know when you alone will decide, when you will decide with their consultation, when you and they will reach a consensus, and when you can live with whatever they decide. They should also know your criteria for deciding how to decide.

Managing Employee Morale. Too often, morale is seen as something that mysteriously happens. In fact, it can be planned for and managed if the supervisor cares not only about results but about staff satisfaction as well. The effective supervisor knows and cares about staff beyond the producing of results. This means taking an interest in each staff member's professional development beyond the job. For example, a supervisor should be supportive of an employee who is learning new skills for job advancement. It also means being sensitive to a staff member's personal circumstances and adapting work conditions (such as flex-time arrangements), within job expectations, to accommodate those circumstances.

Supervise Through the Staff Group. Most organizations require not only individual effort but group effort to get the job done. Committees, staff meetings, project teams, search committees, and other staff groups are all effective in getting the job done. "Divide-and-conquer" managers are often threatened by collective techniques, but effective supervisors know collective measures are necessary to produce results. Morale is also improved because staff function best when they identify with the work unit and with their colleagues. Staff must feel that they can exert influence not only individually but collectively.

Delegate and Communicate. Most professional staff like to operate with a high degree of autonomy, and if they are properly trained and supervised, high autonomy is ideal. But supervisors who delegate must clearly state expected results and insist on frequent communication. They must also have a very high level of trust in those to whom they delegate. Otherwise delegation is a license for staff to "do their own thing," for good or for ill. In such a situation, delegation quickly becomes laissez-faire supervision.

Support Your Staff. Nothing is more disconcerting to subordinates than to feel their boss will not support them when the chips are down or will not advocate for their best interests. Staff must feel the manager is willing to take risks on their behalf, with students, with administrative colleagues, and with the head administrator. Staff need to know that their supervisor will take their concerns to the institutional decision makers and be supportive whenever possible. Staff also need to know when they will not be supported and why.

Lead by Example. Supervisors who practice "Do as I say, not as I do" are always in trouble. Staff need to know that supervisors' expectations of themselves are consistent with their expectations of their employees. For example, supervisors who preach their commitment to high morale but fail to back up that commitment with resources and personally supportive behaviors will very seldom produce high morale.

Step 4: Evaluate Performance for Results and Morale

The key to effective management of staff is to establish fair, clear, and honest systems of individual and organizational accountability. Unfortunately, the norm is for the supervisor to once a year recount his or her impressions of the employee's performance. In some cases, even this does not happen, so the employee is left with a "no-news-is-good-news" standard or patiently waits for the yearly salary increase as a signal of satisfactory performance.

Staff should know where they stand and whether they are producing the results the organization expects. Evaluation should be a continuous process that includes the yearly performance evaluation. Evaluation should be a two-way street in which the employee gets an opportunity to give feedback to the supervisor, but very few supervisors actually implement these principles. Nonetheless, supervisors should use this approach according to the guidelines below.

Establish Clear Performance Objectives. At least once a year, supervisors and staff should agree on specific performance objectives, within job expectations. The job description should be reviewed and discussed. Additional objectives should be specific and committed to writing. For example, in addition to providing high-quality counseling, the objectives of a counselor might be to improve counseling of minorities, increase short-term therapy and reduce longer-term therapy, conduct outreach programs on selected developmental issues, teach a graduate course in abnormal psychology, and chair a committee on professional standards.

Review Performance Objectives at Least Every Three Months. The supervisor and staff member should review progress on job expectations and performance objectives. Objectives may be revised, dropped, or expanded to meet new conditions. The supervisor should not hesitate to judge progress, or lack thereof, and to offer help and assistance.

Use Multiple Sources of Information for Evaluation. No supervisor has all the direct knowledge of the performance of staff members. Supervisors must rely on others, including colleagues, superiors, subordinates, students, and others. Staff should know what sources of information are used and under what circumstances. For example, managers who supervise staff supervisors should have routine ways of knowing how subordinates evaluate their supervisors.

Tie Performance Evaluations to Reward Systems. To have any substantial meaning, performance evaluations should be tied directly to reward systems, especially salary increases. Employees who get outstanding performance ratings and average salary increases will very quickly read what they believe to be the "real" evaluation and start looking for work elsewhere. Likewise, poor performers who get average salary increases will have no real motivation to improve.

Act Quickly to Correct Poor Performance. Poor performance by new employees should be addressed as soon as possible. This is also true for experienced staff. Immediate feedback is preferred to keeping a list of mistakes and presenting these to the employee all at once. Employees should know of your dissatisfaction as soon as possible, and you should take steps to help the employee improve performance.

Get Rid of Poor Performers, and Do It Right. After every effort has been made to bring poor performers up to acceptable standards, they should be dismissed. However, firing employees is now particularly difficult because the personnel policies of most institutions favor employee rights. Make sure that all appropriate personnel policies are followed when terminating an employee, because failure to do so may make it impossible to get rid of someone, even if you can prove their incompetence. Also, take good notes on all relevant discussions and interactions and inform the staff member, in writing, of your judgment about his or her performance. It is impossible to fire someone without a paper trail. Institutional legal counsel should also be involved from the very beginning, because dismissed staff increasingly tend to seek legal recourse.

Model Good Performance Evaluation Procedures. Ask employees for feedback on your job performance and make that feedback available to your supervisor. In addition to soliciting direct feedback from subordinates, give them an opportunity to provide anonymous feedback as well. Regardless of the trust developed between a supervisor and a subordinate, there may be some things that a subordinate may not want to communicate directly but that need to be said.

Performance evaluation is a very complex subject, and this section has provided a very limited overview. Readers who wish a more comprehensive analysis of performance evaluation should consult Robert D. Brown's forthcoming volume (number 43) of the Jossey-Bass monograph series, *New Directions for Student Services.*

Conclusion

Managing people is the most important thing we do to provide results in our organization. Based on our experience, we have developed a model for supervision that begins with recruiting and selecting the right people for the right job, orienting and training them, supervising them to accomplish high productivity and high morale, and measuring their productivity through effective and fair performance evaluations.

References

Blake, R. R., and Mouton, J. S. *The Managerial Grid.* Houston, Tex.: Gulf, 1964.
Burke, W. W. "Leadership: Is There One Best Approach?" *Management Review,* 1980, *69,* 54–56.
Hersey, P., and Blanchard, K. *Management of Organizational Behavior: Utilizing Human Resources.* Englewood Cliffs, N.J.: Prentice-Hall, 1977.

*A number of groups and individuals are important to the
successful operation of a student affairs unit.*

Managing Important Others

Margaret J. Barr

The student newspaper has just come out. The lead story is
on the need for day care on campus. A young staff member
in housing has organized a group to fight, according to the
paper, "the insensitive administration" on this issue. Your
phone rings and you know it is the president's office calling
to ask what is going on. What should be your response?

A local businessman calls complaining about the number
of bad checks he has received from students enrolled at
your institution. He demands action. What can and should
you do?

A faculty member calls complaining that a fraternity's
pledge program is interfering with students' academic work.
He intends to introduce a resolution at the next faculty
senate meeting to ban all national fraternities on the campus. What, if anything, should you do?

These situations and others like them are a part of the daily world
of student affairs administration. Your skill as an administrator lies in
your ability to successfully manage them. The task is not easy, for many
people expect their situations to be handled in a manner satisfactory to
them. The people, the environment, and the processes of higher educa-

M. L. Upcraft and M. J. Barr (eds.). *Managing Student Affairs Effectively.*
New Directions for Student Services, no. 41. San Francisco: Jossey-Bass, Spring 1988.

tion all contribute to situations where confusion, misunderstanding, and miscommunication flourish.

Higher education has been described as political (Barr and Keating, 1985), as organized anarchy (Baldridge, 1971), as difficult to manage (Walker, 1979), and as an entity that is unclear about decision-making processes and procedures (Richman and Farmer, 1974). All these statements are true, as are countless other descriptions of the higher education enterprise, because higher education is basically a human process that relies on communication and problem solving to accomplish the goal of educating students. In a system that is people-intensive, boundless opportunities for problems and conflict arise.

Within such an environment, we as student affairs professionals have special responsibilities. Some view student affairs units as the institutional conscience (Monat, 1985); others view them as the controllers of student behavior. Still others are not at all sure what the unit's role is in the enterprise. With such differing expectations and confusion about our role and function, student affairs administrators must work particularly hard to build effective working relationships with others. Both within and outside the institution, there are a number of key individuals and groups that must be taken into account in policy development, program planning, and day-to-day operations and decisions. Failure to recognize these key groups and individuals and to understand their interest in our work invites disaster and program failure.

This chapter identifies key constituency groups and individuals of special concern to student affairs professionals. Suggestions for opening up communication and breaking down barriers among key constituency groups are presented. The chapter concludes with a discussion of the political environment of higher education and presents guidelines for managing important others.

Chapter One reviewed the general context of American higher education and the complexity of managing the student affairs organizations. An effective student affairs administrator must be able to work with many different groups and individuals who feel that they have a special relationship to the higher education enterprise. If student affairs administrators are not able to establish positive working relationships with and among those who influence the institution, either positively or negatively, then major problems may develop. Many individuals and groups must be accounted for in both policy formation and program development. Thus, it is essential that key constituency groups and individuals be identified and methods developed to work with them.

Managing Key Constituency Groups

A complete list of key individuals and constituency groups for student affairs administrators could be very long. There are a number of people who legitimately feel that they hold a stake in the enterprise of higher education and have specific agendas for student affairs.

Students. Students are the largest and the most diverse constituency group for student affairs. Within any student body, there are some students with specific agendas for student affairs and others who do not even know that we exist. Most students see student affairs divisions not as a distinct organizational entity, but as a series of discrete organizational entities that become important only when such services directly influence their lives or when a student affairs administrator must promulgate or enforce institutional policies. Keeping communication lines open with students is crucial to the success of any student affairs organization. Unless the student affairs administrator can understand the needs of students and effectively translate those needs to others within the organization, students may not receive appropriate services and programs.

It is a mistake, however, to assume that all students are alike and share the same interest on any issue. Sometimes the mistake is made of listening to a few and assuming that they accurately reflect the feelings of the many. To be sure, there are some key groups within the student body that must be identified, and ways must be developed to communicate with them. On some campuses, the student government is one such group. On others, the key group is the governing system for fraternities and sororities. On still others, it is the graduate student organization or the commuter council. The demographics and interests of the student body will define which organized groups are most important for ongoing communication.

Effective methods for maintaining communication with such groups vary from campus to campus. Monthly meetings with key student leaders can be instituted on some campuses. Regular informal dinners are useful on others. It is most effective when the administrator demonstrates willingness to go to student meetings when invited. Whatever the method chosen, care and attention must be given to creating opportunities for genuine discussion and dialogue with key student leaders.

Meeting and maintaining communication with student leaders is not enough. The higher the administrative post you hold within the organization, the less apt you are to have contact with "everyday" students and to appreciate their ups and downs, their successes and their failures. To be an effective student affairs administrator, you must find ways to keep in touch with at least some students on an individual basis. Sometimes this means solving a problem with a student. It often means being present at student events. One of the most effective methods is simply to spend time where students are: at the cafeteria, the student center, or the library. As a famed baseball philosopher once said, "You can learn a lot by just watching." Isolation from students must be fought. An effective administrator creates opportunities to contact and learn to know students and to be known by them. You must determine what will work best on your campus and give it priority status within your busy days. As a student affairs administrator, you must have an intuitive sense of where students are, anticipate their problems, and be able to advocate for student interests where needed and appropriate.

William Monat (1985, p. 57) describes a central responsibility of student affairs, noting that "the professional not be reluctant to speak up on behalf of student interests but never speak down to the student." This is an appropriate expectation of student affairs professionals, but in order to meet it, you must know students in a real and genuine way.

Faculty. I recently participated in a conference in New Mexico entitled "Faculty and Student Affairs: Friends or Foes?" The title and topic reflect how many student affairs professionals view faculty: Faculty are either for us or against us. The reality of the situation does not support such a dichotomous point of view. All faculty, just as all student affairs administrators, do not feel, act, or respond alike. In addition, faculty live in a different world than do student affairs professionals. Reward systems, expectations of performance, and problem solving are all different (Barr and Fried, 1981).

Just because there are differences, however, does not mean faculty should be ignored. In fact, not taking faculty into account can be a fatal error for any student affairs program. To many, the faculty *is* the college or university, a perception that has been relatively constant since medieval times. Student affairs, in contrast, is a relatively new addition to the academy, and thus its role and function is often unclear to faculty.

For the most part, faculty do not think much about student affairs. However, when fiscal resources are tight, faculty budget groups begin to look at student affairs units as a possible source of funding relief. Student affairs programs are often cut because we have not done a good job of explaining to the faculty what we do, why we do it, and what differences there would be on campus if student affairs programs were not present. In order to avoid budget cut battles, an intentional effort must be made to establish ongoing communication with key faculty members and groups.

Some relatively simple approaches seem to work. First, take the initiative to meet with faculty serving on committees directly related to student affairs. Faculty appreciate being informed and having appropriate background information. Training may also need to be offered to faculty serving for the first time on judicial bodies or other quasi-judicial groups.

Second, attend faculty events. Departmental lectures, seminars, and other opportunities occur all the time. Make time to interact with faculty about their interests. In addition to learning something, you will also build bridges for future problem solving if necessary.

Third, if faculty governance groups are open, attend them. You will learn a great deal about their concerns and may have an opportunity to clear up misconceptions or provide information.

Fourth, be available for consultation and assistance when a faculty member is concerned with an individual student. Provide information to aid faculty in referring students, and if students are referred, make sure the faculty member knows something is being done about the problem. You can maintain communication with faculty about individual students and still not break the bonds of confidentiality.

Fifth, be prepared to answer questions about the activities within your units. Know your facts, figures, and what is going on. Preparation and knowledge aid in breaking down communication barriers when they do occur.

Sixth, take faculty concerns seriously. The concerns of the faculty usually become institutional concerns. As a member of the administrative team, you should be an advocate for the entire institution, not just for your own area.

Seventh, create opportunities to involve faculty in the work of student affairs. Faculty fellow programs in residence halls, lectures, service projects, and the like can provide a means for faculty to interact with students and to better understand your work.

Eighth, spend time with faculty. Try to develop opportunities for informal interaction between you and your staff and members of the faculty. This may mean joining faculty for lunch in the faculty center or dropping in where faculty gather informally. It is much more difficult for faculty to assume an adversarial stance with known individuals it is with a faceless administration.

Ninth, when possible, and if you meet the qualifications, try to obtain a faculty appointment. The experience of getting into the classroom helps you more fully understand the faculty perspective of the campus.

Other Administrative Staff. Other administrative staff comprise a key constituency group that is often overlooked within the institution. In addition to student affairs, there are a number of key personnel in business and administrative services on campus who can either assist or thwart you in achieving your objectives. Often these individuals also feel that they are not valued in the enterprise. They tend to look at the world differently, their focus being on their particular administrative function. These individuals can teach you a great deal about how to get something done within the institutional bureaucracy. Take time to understand policies and procedures that affect their area of responsibility. And if you do not understand or feel you can accomplish your objectives within the current rules, enlist their help in solving problems. It is a fatal error to ignore established procedures, for good ideas can be quickly blocked on procedural grounds. Whether the issue is purchasing or maintenance, other administrative staff are key in solving problems.

Again, some relatively simple approaches seem to work best. First, do not assume that because it was done one way in your previous institution that the same procedures prevail in your current assignment. Ask questions and learn how to get things done within your current environment.

Second, if a pattern of problems has developed between your agency and another, sit down and talk about it. Perhaps staff training is needed. Or it may be that the student affairs staff has not clearly articulated their needs. Usually problems can be solved if given sufficient time and attention.

Third, keep other agencies informed. In your planning process, try to determine what influence your decisions will have on other offices and agencies and then, before plans are finalized, discuss them with key decision makers in the other agency. The old adage that people support what they help create is never more true than when working with other administrative officers. Failure to communicate early can lead to untold problems down the road.

Fourth, be supportive. This appears to be a relatively simple idea, but it requires that you understand the pressures and problems others are facing. Perhaps there are ways through cooperative efforts to mutually solve problems.

Staff members in other areas of the university, including the business office, maintenance, or the computer center, can either "make" or "break" student affairs programs. In addition, these individuals have a great deal of contact with students. If you establish good relationships with them, there is a distinct possibility that you can increase their effectiveness in their day-to-day contact with students.

Parents and Family Members. The role that parents and family members will play in your administrative operation will vary from institution to institution. Independent and smaller institutions appear to have more organized and directional contact with parents and family members than do their large public counterparts. However, no matter what the institutional type and purpose, student affairs administrators are usually in contact with this important constituency group.

Parents and family members present both challenges and opportunities for the student affairs administrator. Often the contact comes through some type of crisis faced by the student. Usually, family members are deeply concerned and protective of the student and want something done to alleviate the perceived problem. To be effective under such circumstances, the student affairs administrator must listen effectively and try to sort out what the family member wants from the institution. Often we will not be able to resolve the issue to the satisfaction of family members, but at the very least family members should feel they have had a fair hearing of their complaint.

Deal promptly and directly with parents and family members by returning phone calls and answering correspondence as soon as possible. Be sure to provide as much information as you can to aid them in fully understanding the circumstances surrounding their child's problem. On the other hand, you must be cautious and not violate your institution's policy or federal law regarding the confidentiality of student records.

Other contacts with parents and family members come through formal programs such as new student orientation, college nights, and parents' weekends. The astute student affairs administrator actively plans for such events and tries to develop programs and activities to assist parents and family members in supporting their student. Both large and small campuses have had success in improving communication with parents by developing a parents' newsletter. The newsletter should contain articles of interest to parents as well as important dates and deadlines. Newsletters are an effective method of working with parents unless the newsletters are seen as a thinly veiled approach to fund-raising. Some campuses have had success in establishing representative parents' councils to provide advice and evaluation to the institution. These groups can be very effective but only if their role and scope is clearly defined.

Robert Cohen's *Working with the Parents of College Students* (1985) is an excellent edited collection of resources and can help you understand the complexities of working with this key constituency group.

Governing Boards. On some campuses, student affairs administrators rarely have contact with members of the governing board. On other campuses, such interaction is a daily occurrence. Whatever the style, the student affairs administrator needs to understand the role of the governing board on campus and the expectations of board members.

Board members are an important constituency group for student affairs. Often, parents, members of the community, and others will call board members directly regarding incidents where students are involved in the community. These incidents may range from passing bad checks to making noise in the neighborhood. Whatever the complaint, board members should be aware of who to call on campus to get information or to seek assistance.

Trustees are often caught between "the devil and the deep blue sea." They are experiencing changed expectations of their roles and purpose. Walker (1979, p. 130) states that "before the 1960s, for example, boards generally accepted as a major responsibility the interpretation and defense of the university to the public. Since then, many boards seem to feel that their function is to represent the interests of the public in the management of the university." Thus, although governing boards have a special relationship with the institution, they should not be taken for granted.

Usually the chief executive officer will want to know if you have had contact with a member of the governing board. At the very least, you should assume the responsibility of informing others who need to know that a governing board member has made contact. Sometimes board members become intrusive and ask for exceptions to policy or special consideration for family members or friends. When and if such behavior occurs, do not attempt to confront it by yourself. Immediately seek the assistance of the chief executive officer of the institution in resolving the situation. It usually is not the job of the student affairs administrator to work directly with the board. You will need to take direction from your chief executive officer on how to interact with the board. To do less places the administration of the institution in a difficult position.

Community Members. Residents and office holders in the local community are a specialized constituency group. Community members interact frequently with students, and some are bound to feel anger or frustration about these interactions. Their expectation often is that you as a student affairs professional should do something about their problem. Action on your part may be possible and can aid in resolving some disputes. Sometimes, however, community members have unrealistic expectations of institutional personnel. Thus, each student affairs professional should understand what institutional policies are regarding intervention in off-campus disputes such as bad checks and landlord-tenant problems. In addition to knowing the policies, you also need to be able to explain the institution's position in a clear, informed manner. Most often what you need to do is listen and try to help the community member discover ways to solve the problem. Even if you cannot do what they want, listening respectfully to them often clears the air and creates a sense of understanding.

Student affairs administrators also need to help students understand their responsibilities as good neighbors. Communication with neighborhood groups prior to a large campus event can help prepare them. Often, opportunities can be created to include such groups in events so that neighbors are not just passive observers. Many strategies are possible. Each institution will have different approaches for working with the community; some institutions appoint a staff member as a liaison with the community, others decide not to become involved at all when problems arise. Institutional policy must prevail, and the astute administrator understands and works within that framework.

Other Groups. There are a number of other groups external to the institution who have a stake in the higher education enterprise. These include alumni, government agencies, legislators, and business or industry. The involvement of student affairs with these external constituency groups will vary depending on the unique needs of the campus. In all cases, you need to be clear about the expectations of the institution in relationship to these groups. Be informed about who on campus needs to know about requests or queries from such groups. Keep lines of communication open and do not, under any circumstances, promise more than you can deliver.

Two key groups have not been discussed in this section: student affairs staff and your administrative superior. In Chapter Three, Lee Upcraft discusses issues of management of staff in great detail, and the reader is referred to that chapter. Managing your administrative superior requires special skill and attention and is the subject of the next section.

Managing Your Boss

An effective superior-subordinate relationship requires effort from both. The responsibility for effective communication does not lie just with the supervisor but is a two-way street. What follow are some ground rules for working with a boss.

1. *Do not surprise your boss.* No one likes to be surprised, least of all the person who must protect you, your organization, your programs, and your resources on campus. Inform your supervisor of successes and failures.

2. *Involve your boss.* Make sure that your administrative superior knows what you are doing. If problems arise, let your superior know about them and enlist his or her help in finding solutions. Superiors' knowledge, expertise, and skills can aid you in planning and evaluation. Use them!

3. *Use strategic timing.* Each of us has a rhythm and an approach to our work. Your boss is no exception. Become a good observer of your administrative superior. For example, some people function extremely well under pressure, and you can approach them with anything at any time. For others, a pressured time is absolutely the worst time to approach them with an idea for change or innovation. Observe past successes, ask for advice, and pick up clues to hone your timing skills (see Barr, 1985, pp. 76–77).

4. *Do good staff work.* Try to get explicit direction on what your boss needs to know. Spend time preparing reports and information so that they can be of maximum use to your administrative superior. If you do not provide what your boss wants the first time, learn from the experience so that you can do a better job in the future. Sound staff work builds more bridges of communication with administrative superiors than does any other single thing.

5. *Be faithful.* Being faithful is essential to good communication with your boss and is also an important ethical principle in all of our professional conduct (Kitchener, 1985). Being faithful involves demonstrating loyalty and trustworthiness. Operationally it means not engaging in

gossip about your administrative superior, confronting inaccurate information and perceptions, and trying to demonstrate honesty and integrity. Sometimes there is the opportunity to choose the administrative superior; at other times that decision is made by someone else in the organization. However the relationship starts, you owe your superior your faithfulness; if you cannot be faithful, remove yourself from the organization.

6. *Do not assume you understand everything affecting your boss.* Administrative superiors are people, too, and face all the pressures, problems, and issues that you do. There may be personal issues influencing their work. There may be organizational budget or personal problems influencing their responses. Accord your boss the courtesy of not making assumptions about how he or she behaves. Try instead to be an effective listener and a good communicator. Such personal courtesy and respect will go a long way in developing effective working relationships.

Becoming a Good Campus Politician

Politics is a word that often brings images of smoke-filled rooms, payoffs, and trade-offs. Being political does not have to be a negative stance. It can help in managing and developing open lines of communication with key constituency groups. Although Walker (1979) states that a political view is not the only way to observe and interact with the institution, it can provide a useful perspective for the student affairs professional. Since politics is a part of higher education, the astute professional learns responsible politics as one method for achieving resolution on issues and managing the inevitable conflict within the institution.

Student affairs professionals usually come from a background that places emphasis on interpersonal skill development, and use of interpersonal skills helps individuals and groups grow and develop. This perception often causes barriers when dealing with organizational conflict. Kantor and Stein (1979, p. 306) state that "political issues are not the same as interpersonal issues." Therefore, when we confuse political and interpersonal conflict, we get into trouble. Being a responsible campus politician requires more than just caring and relating. Three additional elements must be accounted for: demonstrating respect, gathering information, and learning to observe and analyze both individual and organizational behavior patterns.

Demonstrating Respect. The politically astute student affairs professional should exhibit respect for every individual and group associated with the institution. Demonstrating respect means taking time to understand why an individual or agency is responding in a certain way. Information must be shared, questions answered, and bases touched on a regular basis. Each agency, department, or division within an institution has a history or tradition. Generally, the agency or department was organized to meet a specific need and is staffed by individuals with expertise in the area. This background, knowledge, and expertise must be respectfully acknowledged in interactions although you may not always agree with the specific point of view being expressed.

On a personal level, political respect is expressed by careful attention to issues of professional protocol and personal courtesy. Whether interacting with a student, staff member, parent, or the most powerful member of the academic organization, recognition of that individual's position and feelings is essential. A useful perspective is often gained by asking yourself, "How would I feel in his or her place?"

Finally, demonstrating respect implies that we recognize and acknowledge the multiple pressures faced by colleagues, students, supporters, and opponents. Listening carefully and openly often is the first step to reaching a decision.

Gathering Information. Seeking and analyzing information is an essential skill for a political manager. There are many sources of information within a college or university. Your skill lies in your ability to separate fact from rumor and speculation. Some information is acquired in casual conversation, although such information usually requires independent verification. Other information emerges through direct inquiry or guided conversations with significant people in the organization. Sometimes gaining significant information requires you to do "homework" by reading files, annual reports, and institutional data. Multiple information networks are essential for you to be able to get the "big picture" and understand what is going on around you. Remember that the well informed are usually the best prepared in a crisis.

Understanding Behavioral Patterns. Most student affairs professionals are skilled in understanding individual behavioral patterns. We use such knowledge all the time in working with student groups, individual students, staff members, and colleagues.

As a rule, however, we are usually less skilled in understanding organizational behavioral patterns. When we transfer our skill of understanding individual behavioral patterns to an organization, we often encounter problems. We expect to understand the antecedents of the organization's behavior. However, it may not be possible or even productive to attempt to reach such an understanding. It is more important to realize that patterns do exist and that elements or issues that appear independent are often linked, if only through the history of the organization.

For example, a director of a health service decided to make a proposal to require mandatory health insurance for all students. She had done her homework, provided a well-reasoned proposal, and was noted for her professional courtesy and tact, yet she could not even get a hearing on her idea as she was making her proposal. The reason can be found in the events that were in progress as she made her proposal: The personnel manager had just informed the executive cabinet that employee health insurance rates were going to rise astronomically. The vice-president for student affairs was attempting to get a number of staff persons reclassified. The president had just received another letter from a parent complaining about the high cost of the institution. Students were raising questions about the increase in tuition rates. While none of these issues directly dealt with student insurance, all were related to cost. No wonder no action was taken on her proposal. The organization needed to sort out what costs were appropriate and only then would a proposal for mandatory insurance be really heard and fairly evaluated.

Responsible political behavior should be part of the expectations of student affairs professionals. Failure to recognize that politics are a part of higher education will result in conflict and unnecessary confusion.

Conclusions and Guidelines for Practice

Management involves working with people. For student affairs administrators, managing important others is key to the success of the student affairs enterprise. The following guidelines will aid you in this task:

1. *Understand your institution.* Each college or university is unique. The distinctive mission, history, and tradition of the institution has a profound influence on the day-to-day management of student affairs programs. The effective manager spends time and energy learning how things are done within the organization. From that basis of understanding, managers can then begin to forge substantive working relationships to accomplish their tasks.

2. *Identify key constituency groups.* On every campus there are numbers of key individuals and groups critical to the success of the academic program. The effective manager quickly identifies these individuals and groups and then opens up communication with them. The techniques and approaches will vary from campus to campus, but the need to establish effective working relationships is always present.

3. *Take the initiative.* Do not wait for others to come to you; seize the initiative. For each constituency group, there are many opportunities to acquaint members with the philosophy, programs, and policies of student affairs. Use your imagination and take some risks. The better you are known, the less likely you will be misunderstood.

4. *Recognize the political environment.* Politics permeate higher education. Being political is not necessarily bad and can be effective in making sure your programs and services are understood.

5. *Do your homework.* Take the time to investigate the background of a problem. Understand that things are not always what they seem to be. If you have done your homework, you will be much better prepared to deal with problems as they arise.

6. *Treat people with respect.* Even if you are not in agreement on

position or tactics, treat each individual with respect. Such a stance opens up rather than closes down communication.

7. *Acknowledge pressures.* All of us have known and unknown pressures in our lives. The effective administrator acknowledges that such pressures are present and does not make assumptions about the motives of others.

8. *Listen carefully and often.* Do not rely on a few people to give you a picture of what is going on. Establish multiple contacts and listen carefully to both what people are saying and what they are not.

9. *Keep in touch.* Even if there is not a pressing problem or concern, it is in the best interest of the institution for you to keep in touch both informally and formally with members of key constituency groups. You will better understand their environment, and your attention will acknowledge the importance of any group to the enterprise.

10. *Understand expectations.* Each group or individual relating to student affairs has expectations of you for action and response. Understanding those expectations is the first step in avoiding communication breakdowns.

All of these guidelines have a common theme: investing time and energy in people. If you do so as a priority, problems can be avoided. This chapter opened with three typical problems faced by a student affairs administrator. Ideally, if these problems occurred, you probably should not have been surprised by any of them. If you are, then there are some things you can immediately do to alleviate problems. Open and caring communication is the first step.

References

Baldridge, J. V. *Power and Conflict in the University.* New York: Wiley, 1971.

Barr, M. J. "Internal and External Forces Influencing Programming." In M. J. Barr, L. A. Keating, and Associates (eds.), *Developing Effective Student Services Programs: Systematic Approaches for Practitioners.* San Francisco: Jossey-Bass, 1985.

Barr, M. J., and Fried, J. "Facts, Feelings, and Academic Credit." In J. Fried (ed.), *Education for Student Development.* New Directions for Student Services, no. 15. San Francisco: Jossey-Bass, 1981.

Barr, M. J., Keating, L. A., and Associates. *Developing Effective Student Services Programs: Systematic Approaches for Practitioners.* San Francisco: Jossey-Bass, 1985.

Brubacher, J. S., and Rudy, W. *Higher Education in Transition.* (rev. ed.) New York: Harper & Row, 1958.

Cohen, R. D. (ed.). *Working with the Parents of College Students.* New Directions for Student Services, no. 32. San Francisco: Jossey-Bass, 1985.

Kantor, R. M., and Stein, B. A. *Life in Organizations.* New York: Basic Books, 1979.

Keller, G. *Academic Strategy: The Management Revolution in American Higher Education.* Baltimore, Md.: Johns Hopkins University Press, 1983.

Kitchener, K. S. "Ethical Principles and Ethical Decisions in Student Affairs." In

64

H. J. Canon and R. D. Brown (eds.), *Applied Ethics in Student Services.* New Directions for Student Services, no. 30. San Francisco: Jossey-Bass, 1985.

Monat, W. R. "Role of Student Services: A President's Perspective." In M. J. Barr, L. A. Keating, and Associates (eds.), *Developing Effective Student Services Programs: Systematic Approaches for Practitioners.* San Francisco: Jossey-Bass, 1985.

Richman, B. M., and Farmer, R. N. *Leadership, Goals, and Power in Higher Education: A Contingency and Open-Systems Approach to Effective Management.* San Francisco: Jossey-Bass, 1974.

Walker, D. E. *The Effective Administrator: A Practical Approach to Problem Solving, Decision Making, and Campus Leadership.* San Francisco: Jossey-Bass, 1979.

Managing "right" requires judgment about conflicting interests, based on management ethics, personal values, and intuition.

Managing Right

M. Lee Upcraft

Your staff and colleagues agree that you should hire their first choice as a director of residence halls, but your instinct tells you their second choice is really the best candidate. What is the right choice?

In order to avoid another tuition increase, your institution has frozen all staff salaries at current levels. Your staff is very upset. What is the right way to handle the situation?

You and your staff favor a student activities fee because you believe the increased income generated will be in the best interests of the students. Your boss is opposed to such a fee in the interests of keeping overall costs down. What is the right thing to do?

Your students are strongly opposed to disciplinary sanctions for on-campus underage drinking. You believe students should be held accountable for behavior that is illegal. What is the right course of action?

Each of these dilemmas is difficult to manage right because as managers we must make decisions and develop policies that at once serve

M. L. Upcraft and M. J. Barr (eds.). *Managing Student Affairs Effectively.*
New Directions for Student Services, no. 41. San Francisco: Jossey-Bass, Spring 1988.

the best interests of students, staff, and the institution while remaining true to accepted management ethics, our own sense of values, and our intuitive judgment. Balancing all elements is rarely easy, and most of our decisions are of the "no-win" variety.

This chapter identifies some of the dilemmas of managing "right," and suggests how managers should proceed when the best interests of staff, students, and the institution are in conflict. The chapter also identifies the management ethics, personal values, and intuitive judgment necessary to manage right and points out ways to minimize conflict and resistance.

Mission Impossible: Managing in the Best Interests of Everyone

Most good managers would readily concede that one of their major responsibilities is to make decisions and develop policies that serve the best interests of students, staff, and the institution. Most good managers would also admit that this task is rarely easy and that most decisions and policies fall short of the best interests of all three, in spite of the manager's best intentions. Managing under such circumstances is often agonizing, difficult, and puts the manager in a no-win position.

Managing in the Best Interests of Students. It is easy for us to say that we as student services professionals serve the best interests of students, advocate on their behalf, and assist them in pursuing their educational and personal goals. After all, that is our purpose. But even if we set aside for the moment some of the problems created by this value for the institution, managing to serve the best interests of students is not simple.

First, how do we know what the best interests of students are? We can assume we know because of our training, experience, and traditional stereotypes of our student body. We can accumulate the collective wisdom of our staff who interact on a daily basis with students. Or in some unsystematic way, we can be guided by student development literature and research.

A more obvious way to find out what is in students' best interests is to ask them. Unfortunately, students themselves may not know what is in their best interests. While we may believe students are adults who can and do articulate their own needs, values, and interests, we also know that what students think they want may not be what they need. A good example is freshman orientation. We may ask freshmen just out of high school what they think they need before they come to college, but in fact, they have very little basis for answering, since they have never been to college before. So we depend on orientation research and literature to determine what we think freshmen really need as opposed to what they think they need.

Even if we have a good idea of what the best interests of all students are, we may have conflicting student interests. What benefits one group of students may not benefit another. At small, single-purpose institutions that attract a more homogeneous student body, the question of what is in students' best interests may be easily answered. But for most institutions, there is too much diversity among students to provide a single answer to this question.

Owing to limited resources, most managers spend a lot of time and anguish sorting out priorities among the competing best interests of several different student subgroups. Very often this means that when we act in the best interests of one student group, it is at the expense of another student group. A good example is the allocation of resources for student organizations. To compensate for new student organizations that develop, which student organizations that already have resources should no longer be funded? Or should all existing organizations be reduced to fund new student organizations? Or should fees be raised to accommodate the new group?

Another example is the creation of special programs to meet the needs of student subpopulations, such as ethnic minorities, women, the disabled, adult learners, veterans, and others. How do we decide which of these many student populations will be served by separate programs and which ones will be directed to "mainstream" student services? If we create special programs for these groups, must resources for mainstream student services be reduced?

So how do we determine what is in the best interests of students? At a minimum, we must develop systematic ways of assessing student needs and outcomes, following these guidelines:

1. *Identify the characteristics of your students.* Look at demographic, background, attitudinal, economic, educational, and other characteristics of your students and compare these with other similar institutional and national norms. You should be able to describe your student body as they enter your institution and as they matriculate toward graduation.

2. *Conduct studies of student needs and satisfactions with services.* You should know your students' interpersonal, social, academic, spiritual, vocational, health, and other developmental needs. Devise your own surveys or use nationally normed instruments. Periodically ask students if they use your services and if they are satisfied with those services. Make sure such studies are differentiated by gender, race, age, and other variables that can affect needs and satisfactions.

3. *Know student development theory and published research.* You should know student development theory and be relatively current with published research on student needs, academic achievement, and personal development.

4. *Spend time with your staff discussing student needs.* "Firing-line" staff who spend significant amounts of time with students can be helpful in assessing needs, describing characteristics, and identifying problems and issues of students. Too often, we do not take the time to listen to these staff, but they have much to offer managers who spend less time with students.

5. *Spend time with students.* Many managers, particularly those in higher administrative positions, do not systematically spend time with students. If they do, the time is likely to be task or problem oriented or be spent with a very unrepresentative sample of students, such as student leaders. You need to take time to talk with students about their needs, concerns, problems, and issues and to make sure that all groups in the student body are represented.

6. *Follow professional ethical standards in dealing with students.* For example, the Council for the Advancement of Standards (CAS) for Student Services/Development Programs' *Standards and Guidelines for Student Services/Development Programs* (1986) includes ethical statements on confidentiality, human subjects, nondiscrimination, and other issues relevant to staff-student relationships. Similar ethical statements are contained in the National Association of Student Personnel Administrators' (NASPA) "Standards of Professional Practice" and the American College Personnel Association's (ACPA) "Statement of Ethical and Professional Standards" (1985).

Managing in the Best Interests of the Institution. All student services professionals have an ethical duty to conduct themselves within the mission, goals, and values of the institution for which they work. They also have a duty to question those values, attempt to change them, and, when they cannot change them, live with them or leave. But for the most part, when we work in an institution, we have some sense that what we value is consistent with the values of the institution. But as with managing in the best interests of students, managing in the best interests of the institutions is not simple.

Identifying the best interests of the institution is not easy. At smaller, more single-purpose institutions where values may be more clear, the best interests of the institution may be easier to identify. But in larger, multipurpose institutions, institutional best interests may be more elusive. For example, quality may be valued regardless of cost. Or quality may be sacrificed to maintain enrollments. Or the institution's best interests may be serving critical outside interests, such as legislatures, alumni, or corporate donors. Or the needs of the faculty may predominate, as is sometimes the case in large, research-oriented graduate institutions.

Whatever the definition of the "best interests of the institution," (and for most institutions, it is probably a combination of the above-mentioned interests), student services managers must be aware of and manage in a way that serves these interests. The following guidelines can be of help:

1. *Know your institution.* Know what your institution really values and rewards. For example, in large research universities, published research and corporate collaboration may be valued over teaching and community service. At institutions where enrollments are declining, retention may be the predominant value. At institutions where money is scarce, cost effectiveness may be the bottom line.

2. *Know the people in your institution.* To a great extent, people within the institution define its best interests. Knowing how the president, the vice-presidents, department heads, the faculty senate, and others in positions of power define institutional best interests is very important. It is especially important to know how your boss defines institutional best interests, because he or she will have a direct impact on your services and programs.

3. *Know the external influences on your institution.* In public institutions, you must know where the money comes from and what the money providers, such as state legislatures and federal agencies, expect of your institution. In private institutions, you must know about the pressures from alumni, corporate and other donors, state and federal governments, and religious denominations.

These pressures are real. Recent examples include legislative efforts to establish competency examinations and the many restrictions on federal and state grants and corporate gifts. A most blatant and recent example was the successful effort of a major corporate donor to a leading private institution to temporarily block the admission of a graduate student who worked for a competitor.

4. *Know your ethical obligations to your institution.* For example, the NASPA "Standards of Professional Practice" include an ethical commitment on the part of student affairs professionals to agree with institutional goals and missions and to respect the legal and social codes and moral expectations of the communities in which they live and work. The Council for the Advancement of Standards' general standards also apply.

If you know these things, you will be in a better position to know what the best interests of the institution are and how to take them into account in managing right.

Managing in the Best Interests of Student Services Staff. A third constituency to be taken into account in managing right is the student services staff. Since high productivity and staff morale are the two major goals of management, we must take into account their best interests in managing right. Once again, this is not easy. First, staff are diverse and may not have common interests. Counselors may have different needs than residence hall staff, who in turn have different needs than health care providers. Particularly in larger institutions where student services are more specialized, it may be very difficult to serve the best interests of all staff.

Second, student affairs staff sometimes feel that their best interests get third billing after the institution and students. They may get this feeling based on budget allocations or consistent failure to get across to the institution a student development point of view.

How does one manage staff to serve their best interests? Basically by managing in the ways suggested in Chapter Four, including the appropriate recruiting, selecting, orienting, training, supervising, and evaluating of staff. But the following are also useful managerial guidelines:

1. *Make sure staff opinions are taken into account in the decision making and policy development of student affairs and of the institution.* You need staff opinions if you are to adequately represent their best interests. Also, staff will be more able to accept a decision that does not seem to be in their direct best interests if they have had adequate input and feel that their point of view has been heard.

2. *Let staff know the reasons for a decision or policy.* Staff need to know the outcome of their input and the reasons for a decision or policy. Again, they will be more likely to accept an adverse policy or decision if they understand the reasons for it.

3. *Consider direct ways of assessing staff needs.* Too often, we rely on the administrative hierarchy to identify staff needs. A natural filtering process occurs that may dilute and prejudice the real feelings of staff. This problem may be surmounted by conducting personal interviews or written surveys asking about such issues as job satisfaction or professional development needs.

Student affairs staff need to be part of the best interests triangle and to know that student affairs managers are looking out for the staff's best interests as well as those of the students and the institution.

Conflicts of Interests

Managing in the best interests of students, the institution, and staff inevitably leads the manager to make decisions based on the "greatest good for the greatest number," that is, no-win decisions. Very rarely can all three be satisfied.

The best interests of students often conflict with the best interests of the institution, and this often poses the most difficult dilemma for the chief student services officer as an advocate for their best interests within the institution. On the other hand, the president will inevitably look to the chief student services officer and his or her staff as the advocate for the best interests of the institution with students.

There are countless examples of student-institutional conflict. Should tuition be raised to protect the quality of programs and services or kept the same to preserve students' ability to pay the costs of their education? Should the institution divest holdings in South Africa, making a statement against apartheid, or maintain investments to protect the fiduciary integrity of the institution? Should AIDS testing be required for entering students, thus helping to protect the general public health, or should testing be optional, thus preserving the civil liberties of AIDS victims?

There are also many examples of student-staff conflicts. Should tuition be raised to make possible competitive staff increases? Should evening hours for selected student services be made available to students, thereby creating inconvenient working hours for staff? Should student assessments of services and programs be staff specific? Should student opinions prevail over staff opinions?

Staff-institutional conflict can also occur. Should staff salaries be frozen and benefits limited to ensure the fiscal integrity of the institution? May staff members take public stands in opposition to institutional policies?

Or two of the three constituencies can be in conflict with the third. Students and staff may be aligned in favor of divesting holdings in South Africa, while the institution may be firmly against such divestment. Staff and the institution may align against students on tuition increases. And there are many other examples.

What should the student services manager do when the best interests of students, staff, and the institution are in conflict? The following guidelines can be of help:

1. *Consider your role in the conflict.* Sometimes you must advocate for the institutional position, particularly if you are the chief student affairs officer. Sometimes you are free to advocate for the student position, if that position is clear, to choose one student position over another, or to choose a staff position. Sometimes you can serve as a mediator or problem solver. But whatever role you have, it should be clear to everyone just what you are doing and why, because your role may change from issue to issue.

2. *Make sure that all sides understand each other.* Even if you are committed to the institutional position on an issue, you can still help the other sides understand the issue and the position each has taken. For example, if a tuition increase has been proposed, the administration and governing board must understand the impact of rising tuition on students' financial survival. Students, on the other hand, must understand the fiscal realities of the institution and the consequences of not raising tuition. The student affairs manager has a responsibility to ensure that each side understands all that is involved in the issue.

3. *Help your staff determine their role.* Staff, too, need to know what role they might assume in an institution-student conflict. They

may have to support the institutional stance, be available for mediation, or be free to advocate for students or themselves. In any event, the staff should know their roles and the consequences of their actions.

4. *Know the institution's tolerance for dissent.* If there is freedom to dissent from the institution's best interests, the limitations and consequences of that position must be clear. Often students have greater latitude to dissent from institutional decisions than staff, but even so there are consequences for students, including their continued credibility with institutional decision makers. There is sometimes greater tolerance for staff closest to students to advocate on their behalf and much less tolerance for chief student affairs officers to do so. Sometimes there is little tolerance for public advocacy and great tolerance for behind-the-scenes, internal dissent. Sometimes there is great tolerance for dissent before a decision is made and very little thereafter. In any event, staff and students should understand how much tolerance there is for dissent and under what conditions it is appropriate and the consequences of such action.

5. *Be prepared to take a stand.* Although there may be some instances where you should avoid taking a stand (such as when you are in a mediating role), it is probably best in the long run that students, the institution, and your staff know where you stand and why. Ultimately, this involves making your best judgment about the best interests of all three, based on consideration of all variables and your own values.

In summary, managing conflicts of interests among students, the institution, and staff is never easy because serving the best interests of all three is seldom possible. We may oppose, support, mediate, or compromise, depending on the situation, institutional tolerance for our actions, and our own values. The trick is to make sure that everyone (staff, students, and the institution) clearly understands which tactic we are choosing and why.

Management Ethics

The advice offered so far will work only if the manager is making decisions in an ethical manner. We agree with Kitchener (1985, p. 18) that "ethical decision making is always a matter of a particular situation and that the facts of that situation dictate the ethical rules, ethical principles, and ethical theories that have relevance for a decision." However, we also agree with her that certain ethical principles do apply to a manager's decision making, including:

1. *Respecting autonomy.* One should manage in a way that respects people's right to decide how to live their lives as long as their actions do not interfere with the welfare of others.

2. *Doing no harm.* One should not manage in a way that runs a high risk of harming others either physically or psychologically.

3. *Benefiting others.* One should manage in a way that promotes student intellectual, moral, and personal development, while doing no harm and respecting their autonomy.

4. *Being just.* One should manage in a way that treats people fairly and with impartiality, equality, and reciprocity, recognizing that equal treatment may not result in an equal outcome for everyone.

5. *Being faithful.* One should manage in a way that commits to loyalty, truthfulness, promise keeping, and respect.

If these principles are adhered to, managing the best interests of students, the institution, and staff will not only be easier, it will be done in a way that generates respect for the integrity of the decision-making process and the decision maker.

The Manager's Personal Values

So far, the importance of managing in the best interests of students, the institution, and staff and how to manage when these best interests are in conflict have been discussed as have the ethical principles within which management decisions should be made. However, the initial definition of managing right included the manager's own values. While many personal values could be listed, there are six values that are important in managing right: honesty, fairness, integrity, predictability, courage, and confidentiality.

Honesty. The most damning thing that can be said about a manager is that he or she is dishonest. In organizational settings, dishonesty is more often a matter of omission than of commission. That is, very few managers lie outright about something. More often, dishonesty is a result of what is not said rather than of what is said.

"Half truths" (as seen by the manager) or "half lies" (as seen by others) are always trouble, even if they are well intended. Sometimes managers do not tell the whole truth because they want to avoid hurting others' feelings or unpleasant or confrontational interactions. But avoiding telling the whole story is a losing strategy, because eventually the whole truth comes out and the manager is not only condemned for the decision but for being dishonest.

Half truths should be distinguished, however, from legitimate organizational constraints on information or projected decisions. All managers have information that cannot be shared or can be shared only with limited audiences, in general terms, or at some future time. Honesty can be maintained in these instances by simply stating the constraints, the reasons for those constraints, and projecting a timetable for further information.

Fairness. Being fair means dealing with management issues in an open, nonprejudicial way. If the best interests of the student, the institution, and the employee are in conflict, the even handedness of the manager is important. This means not making up your mind in advance of the discussion. It also means hearing and understanding the points of view of all sides. Controversial decisions are much easier to defend if all sides feel the manager has dealt with them fairly, even if they think the outcome was unfair.

Integrity. Having integrity means having a consistency between beliefs and actions. "Talking a good game" is easy, but acting on those beliefs is yet another matter. Managers who establish a reputation as "all show and no go" will soon go out the door. It may be basic advice, but managers should never say anything they do not mean. They should avoid platitudes that will later come back to haunt them, or worse yet, platitudes that can be interpreted in multiple ways. Saying one thing and doing another or not doing anything at all is a monumental mistake if one wants to maintain integrity.

For example, it is easy for a manager to give lip service to staff morale. It takes more effort and integrity, however, to allocate resources to promote staff development or to take the time to recognize in visible ways the outstanding performance of employees. Integrity is judged by consistency between words and deeds, not just by words.

Predictability. Closely related to fairness and integrity is predictability. That is, do you act consistently from one situation to another or from one decision to another? Can the people that work with you most often predict how you will respond to a given situation, based on your consistent track record in similar situations? There are few things more damaging to a manager's credibility than unpredictability. Unpredictability leads to questions of a manager's honesty, fairness, and integrity and creates tension among those affected.

Courage. Having courage means being willing to make tough decisions and to stand by them when pressures mount. Courage means sticking to decisions or situations because you know you are right. It means being willing to make no-win decisions and not giving in to pressure after decisions are made. It means standing behind employees when they are right. It may mean standing against students, your boss, your staff, or all three. Ultimately, it means you are willing to risk your job for what you believe in.

Confidentiality. Maintaining confidentiality means that you preserve and protect the confidential information available to you as a manager. It means establishing a well-earned reputation of keeping the confidences of everyone you work with and for and resisting the temptation to share confidential information when it may enhance your own ego, status, or power position. Confidentiality should be breached only when there is potential harm to a person or to the general public welfare.

These values, when applied to organizational dilemmas, help managers keep their organizations focused on the issues rather than how the issues were handled or who handled them. These values also ensure that the manager is managing right by maintaining his or her integrity.

Intuitive Judgment

So far, it has been argued that managing right means managers must serve the best interests of students, the institution, and staff and apply management ethics and personal values to situations, policies, and decisions. But the "right" decision may still not be obvious. Some decisions are so complicated that even when all the facts are in, all the people consulted, all the management ethics and personal values applied, the decisions are still too close to call. Or worse yet, from the manager's perspective, he or she may have a "gut feeling" that is contrary to the prevailing opinion. Then what? In these situations all that is left is the manager's intuition and the courage to do what he or she believes is right.

Rowan (1986) believes that really good managers follow their hunches, or intuitions, even when the facts are certain, the ethics and values are sound, and the people agree. He believes that the biggest roadblock to creative management is not having the courage to follow a good hunch. He defines a hunch as "facts plus intuition," or getting your head and your heart working together. He is particularly critical of managers who overanalyze problems and do not utilize their own and others' intuition. Intuitive managers are trial-and-error thinkers who are willing to risk ridicule or failure while following a hunch.

Put more simply, if, after you have done all the considering and consulting and fact gathering you can the decision is still not clear, you should go with your intuition. You will feel better, and the decision will probably be better and be better understood. No one can really argue with the answer: "I considered everything and everybody, and ultimately I had to go with what I *felt* was right."

Managing a Right Decision

Making the right decision is only half the battle. The other half is managing that decision so that it is understood by all those affected and is implemented with your original intent. Many times an unpopular decision, when not managed properly, can be easily subverted. How many times have you responded to a decision you disagreed with by saying to yourself, "How can I get around that one?" Making a right but unpopular decision acceptable to subordinates, colleagues, superiors, and students requires a lot of thought and planning, including:

1. *Testing your decision against institutional values and mission.* You are in a stronger position when your decision is consistent with

institutional values and mission. When you are in conflict with those values and mission, you should reconsider your decision. If you stick to your decision, you must consider the consequences, including resigning or being removed from your position.

2. *Discuss your decision with your boss.* Most bosses do not like surprises; in addition, support from your superior on a controversial decision is critical. If your boss cannot support you, then either you make a decision and take the chance of being overturned or you adjust your decision to accommodate your boss's concerns. Your superior needs to know what your decision will be; the reasons for the decision; the consequences of the decision for students, staff, the institution, and the public; and, most important, the consequences for your boss.

3. *When appropriate, discuss your decision with legal counsel.* In this litigious age, it is especially important to ask your institution's legal counsel to review your projected decision and offer advice on the potential legal complications resulting from it. If a decision could involve litigation, you need to know what your chances are in a lawsuit and if the risk and expense are worth it. On the other hand, just because a decision might result in litigation does not necessarily make it wrong.

4. *Time your decision appropriately.* When it comes to controversial decisions, timing may be everything. Can the institution stand another controversy at this time? Is the political climate conducive to making the decision stick? Are students ready to accept another controversial decision at this time? Is this the issue to "go to the wall" with, or are there others that would be better?

5. *Make sure all persons affected know and understand your decision and the reasons for it.* This may mean sitting down with staff, students, or groups to discuss what you did and why you did it. You do not have to reargue the issue or persuade opponents, but you do want to make sure people understand in advance of any public announcements. People directly affected by a decision should not learn about it for the first time through the media.

6. *Make clear the channels for appeal of your decision, if any.* Sometimes your decision is final, and sometimes the organization or situation allows for an appeal of your judgment. Persons affected should know if there is any appeal and, if so, what those appeal channels are.

7. *Make sure the media understands your decision and the reasons for it.* The media needs to be managed through well-thought-out public releases and, when necessary, press conferences. Most institutions have public information specialists who deal with the media, and these specialists should be involved in planning strategies for public announcements. In general, full disclosure of information about the decision should be the rule, except where confidentiality of personnel, budgets, or students must be protected.

8. *Make clear what you expect of your staff.* Staff who agree with your decision will need some direction in implementing it. Those who disagree will need to know that you expect them to help implement the decision even though they may continue to disagree with it.

9. *Do not tolerate continued resistance by staff after the decision is made.* Managing right means that you gave plenty of opportunity in advance of a decision for those affected to be heard. It also means that resistance by staff after the decision will not be tolerated, and staff should know this. They should also know the consequences of continued resistance up to and including dismissal.

10. *Help staff who cannot accept your decision to consider alternatives.* For most staff on most issues, implementing a decision with which they disagree, while not ideal, is accepted as a basic part of organizational existence. However, occasionally there may be a staff member who simply cannot accept a decision. If this is the case, managing right means helping such persons move on to a job and an organizational setting more consistent with their goals and beliefs.

11. *Be prepared to back off a bad decision.* Perhaps the toughest advice in managing a right decision is to back off if events, situations, and circumstances demonstrate that you made a wrong, bad, or untimely decision. When it is clear that you erred, back off quickly to cut your losses and go back to the drawing board. Admitting you are wrong and reapproaching the whole situation is hard on the ego, but most people can more easily forgive your bad judgment if you back off than if you continue to push a bad decision.

Summary

Managing right means managing in ways that serve the best interests of students, staff, and the institution, consistent with management ethics and the manager's values and intuitive judgment. When best interests conflict, the manager must take action in ways that may range from mediation to taking a stand. A manager must also comply with accepted management ethics, including respecting autonomy, doing no harm, benefiting others, being just, and being faithful. A manager's own values apply as well, including honesty, fairness, integrity, predictability, courage, and confidentiality. And finally, a manager's intuitive judgment may apply in spite of everything else. Managing a right decision is also important if the decision is to have credibility.

References

American College Personnel Association. "Statement of Ethical and Professional Standards." (Appendix 1.) In H. J. Canon and R. D. Brown (eds.), *Applied Ethics in Student Services.* New Directions for Student Services, no. 30. San Francisco: Jossey-Bass, 1985.

78

Council for the Advancement of Standards (CAS) for Student Services/Development Programs. *CAS Standards and Guidelines for Student Services/Development Programs*. Washington, D.C.: Council for the Advancement of Standards, 1986.

Kitchener, K. S. "Ethical Principles and Ethical Decisions in Student Affairs." In H. J. Canon and R. D. Brown (eds.), *Applied Ethics in Student Services*. New Directions for Student Services, no. 30. San Francisco: Jossey-Bass, 1985.

National Association of Student Personnel Administrators. "Standards of Professional Practice." (Appendix 2.) *Applied Ethics in Student Services*. New Directions for Student Services, no. 30. San Francisco: Jossey-Bass, 1985.

Rowan, R. *The Intuitive Manager*. Boston: Little, Brown, 1986.

Selected management references for student affairs professionals are presented in this chapter.

Conclusions and Annotated Bibliography

Margaret J. Barr, M. Lee Upcraft

Management in student affairs is not an easy task. Whether you are the chief student affairs officer or a department head, effective management strategies must be mastered and used to promote quality student services programs. Approaches to management that are effective in a business or industrial setting must be modified to account for the unique governance and decision-making structures within higher education institutions. A strict line staff organization does not prevail, and decisions are usually arrived at through consultation and review. Thus, the effective student affairs manager cannot work in isolation. Student affairs programs are an integral part of the institution and are influenced by the role, mission, policies, and procedures of that institution. Like all members of the college or university community, the student affairs manager must understand and appreciate the influence of the larger society on the educational enterprise. Sensitivity to both internal and external political realities is essential, and responsible political behavior on the part of the manager must be consistently demonstrated. Effective managers in student affairs understand the unpredictability of their work environment and acquire skills and competencies to increase their effectiveness in the management role.

Managers in student affairs must assess and take steps to remedy

M. L. Upcraft and M. J. Barr (eds.). *Managing Student Affairs Effectively.*
New Directions for Student Services, no. 41. San Francisco: Jossey-Bass, Spring 1988.

their own skill deficits. Although organizational issues create barriers to improving managerial effectiveness, such barriers are not insurmountable. Careful attention to questions of power, authority, process, and protocol can assist managers in improving their personal effectiveness and that of the student affairs organization.

Sound management of the fiscal resources of the student affairs organization is essential. The current state of finances in higher education creates conditions where absence of fiscal management and budgetary skills can cause enormous problems for student affairs programs. Funding of and budgeting for student affairs programs is complicated. Multiple sources of funds are used, and an appropriate mix of funding sources must be developed to support the student affairs function. Both short-term and long-term implications of funding and budgeting decisions must be considered. Planning is required not only in fiscal matters but in the design of programs, services, and activities. The productivity and effectiveness of higher education is not easy to measure. Colleges and universities often have ambiguous goals, and this complicates the task of effective management in student affairs. Specific goals should be developed for student affairs programs that relate to and support the mission of the institution. As a result of such goal statements, key decision makers within the institution should be able to tell what will or will not happen if a specific program or service receives either increased or diminished funding.

Effective staff are essential to quality student affairs programs. From the recruitment process to evaluation, student affairs managers must devote time, energy, and resources to personnel management functions. In a labor-intensive enterprise such as student affairs, failure to devote such effort will inevitably cause problems and diminish the effectiveness of the student affairs program.

A number of key constituency groups are important to the success of the student affairs enterprise. Students, other administrators, faculty, staff, parents, alumni, and others external to the institution all have expectations of higher education. Student affairs managers have a special responsibility to ensure that communication and interaction with all key constituency groups and individuals are open, honest, and straightforward. The student affairs manager must take time to understand the expectations of each constituency group and be able to interpret policies, decisions, and practices to those involved in the process.

The managerial environment for student affairs professionals is both volatile and unpredictable. Difficult decisions often must be made, and conflict and disagreement inevitably will arise within the education community. Both the process of decision making and the final decision are important. Competing rights and interests must be carefully balanced within the institution, and discussion and debate must be encouraged.

Although political pressures, personal concerns, politics, and competition for resources are present within the institution, student affairs managers must apply ethical and humane principles in all aspects of their work.

Finally, although this volume has been filled with practical advice and ideas, there is one important ingredient that must not be overlooked, namely, maintaining a sense of humor and perspective. Most of us joined the student affairs profession because of our love of students and our commitment to the educational process. The nature of the population with which we work guarantees that not everything will always go smoothly. Mistakes will be made. Problems will be blown out of proportion. Issues will be magnified. At the same time, however, individual students, staff, and members of student organizations will grow and learn. Progress will be made, and successes will occur. Higher education, with all of its problems and peculiarities, is a challenging and interesting place to work. All of us must keep our sense of humor and perspective, take joy in our day-to-day tasks, and enjoy the unique opportunities we have as we manage the student affairs enterprise.

This sourcebook is not intended to be a scholarly approach to management in student affairs. Instead, it has been a practical guide derived from our own experiences and that of our colleagues around the country. By necessity, a number of issues associated with effective management in student affairs have not been discussed here. It is our hope, however, that we have stimulated your thinking and challenged you to examine your own effectiveness as a manager. If we have done that, we believe that our goal has been met.

The following sources of additional information have been selected because we believe they will provide insight and assistance.

Annotated Bibliography

Baldridge, J. V. *Power and Conflict in the University.* New York: Wiley, 1971.
    This volume provides a cogent analysis of the politics of higher education. Internal and external political pressures are identified, and methods are presented to aid faculty and staff members in mastering the political environment.

Barr, M. J., Keating, L. A., and Associates. *Developing Effective Student Services Programs: Systematic Approaches for Practitioners.* San Francisco: Jossey-Bass, 1985.
    This book analyzes program development in student affairs in terms of context, goal, and plan for such programs. Practical advice is given to help practitioners successfully install student affairs programs within the institution.

Boyer, E. L. *College: The Undergraduate Experience in America.* New York: Harper & Row, 1987.

This volume presents the report of the Carnegie Foundation for the Advancement of Teaching. Analyzing the undergraduate experience in American colleges and universities, it provides a critical analysis of what is right and wrong in undergraduate education and offers suggestions for improvement that are of specific interest to student affairs professionals.

Canon, H. J., and Brown, R. D. (eds.). *Applied Ethics in Student Services.* New Directions for Student Services, no. 30. San Francisco: Jossey-Bass, 1985.

Through case study and applications, this sourcebook brings ethical practices into the daily work of student affairs. The discussion of ethical dilemmas and sources of help are particularly useful.

Delworth, U., Hanson, G. R., and Associates (eds.). *Student Services: A Handbook for the Profession.* San Francisco: Jossey-Bass, 1980.

A comprehensive guide to identifying, assessing, and evaluating student affairs programs, this volume is essential to practitioners. Five major topics are considered: growth and status of student services, theoretical bases of the profession, models for practice, essential competencies, and organization and management.

Hersey, P., and Blanchard, K. *Management of Organizational Behavior: Utilizing Human Resources.* Englewood Cliffs, N.J.: Prentice-Hall, 1977.

In this classic text, Hersey and Blanchard introduce the concept of "situational leadership," or the importance of adapting leadership styles to the situation and the maturity level of the individual or groups to be led. This book is particularly useful to entry-level managers.

Hoy, W. K., and Miskel, C. G. *Educational Administration: Theory, Research, and Practice.* New York: Random House, 1978.

Although focused on elementary and secondary school settings, this volume provides insight for student affairs practitioners. The overviews on theory, decision making, and communication are particularly helpful.

Kantor, R. M., and Stein, B. A. *Life in Organizations.* New York: Basic Books, 1979.

This volume provides insight into what really goes on in organizations. Underlying themes of organizational life are identified, and principles of organizational behavior are articulated.

Keller, G. *Academic Strategy: The Management Revolution in American Higher Education.* Baltimore, Md.: Johns Hopkins University Press, 1983.

Keller's extensive study of current problems and trends in American higher education provides a perspective that is useful for student affairs administrators. His practical advice can be adapted to many organizations.

Lakein, A. *How to Get Control of Your Time and Your Life.* New York: Peter H. Wyden, 1973.

This volume presents a number of practical suggestions on how to become better organized and gain control of your life as a manager. Although all Wyden's suggestions may not work for everyone, some of his suggestions may be helpful.

Radde, P. *Supervising: A Guide for All Levels.* San Diego, Calif.: University Associates, 1981.

A basic handbook of supervision, this book covers decision making from the moment a person is faced with the choice of becoming a supervisor to the decision of whether or not to promote subordinates to supervisory positions. The volume includes topics such as performance appraisals, supervising for results, and supervising the human dimension.

Rowan, R. *The Intuitive Manager.* Boston: Little, Brown, 1986.

This book explains how important "intuitive judgment," or following a hunch, is to management decisions and organizational effectiveness and creativity. Rowan believes intuition can be understood, nurtured, and, above all, trusted and turned into a powerful management tool.

Walker, D. E. *The Effective Administrator: A Practical Approach to Problem Solving, Decision Making, and Campus Leadership.* San Francisco: Jossey-Bass, 1979.

Although by no means a scholarly approach to managing higher education, this volume provides practical insight and wisdom from a presidential perspective. The book is both entertaining and insightful.

Index